# THREE
# ESSAYS
## ON
# RELIGION

Nature
The Utility of Religion
Theism

## JOHN STUART
# MILL

GREAT BOOKS IN PHILOSOPHY

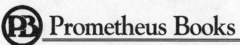 Prometheus Books

59 John Glenn Drive
Amherst, New York 14228-2197

Published 1998 by Prometheus Books

59 John Glenn Drive, Amherst, New York 14228–2197,
716–691–0133. FAX: 716–691–0137.

Library of Congress Cataloging-in-Publication Data

Mill, John Stuart, 1806–1873.
[Essays. Selections]
Three essays on religion : Nature, The utility of religion,
Theism / John Stuart Mill.
    p.    cm. — (Great books in philosophy)
Originally published: Nature, The utility of religion, and The-
ism. London : Longmans, Green, Reader, and Dyer, 1874.
    ISBN 1–57392–212–9 (alk. paper)
    1. Religion—Philosophy. 2. Nature. 3. Theism. I. Mill,
John Stuart, 1806–1873. Nature. II. Mill, John Stuart, 1806–1873.
Utility of religion. III. Mill, John Stuart, 1806–1873. Theism.
IV. Title. V. Series.
BL51.M62     1998
210—dc21                                                    98–15124
                                                                CIP

Printed in the United States of America on acid-free paper.

## Additional Titles on the Philosophy of Religion in Prometheus's Great Books in Philosophy Series

Marcus Tullius Cicero
*The Nature of the Gods* and *On Divination*

Ludwig Feuerbach
*The Essense of Christianity*

David Hume
*Dialogues Concerning Natural Religion*

John Locke
*A Letter Concerning Toleration*

Lucretius
*On the Nature of Things*

Thomas Paine
*The Age of Reason*

Bertrand Russell
*Bertrand Russell on God and Religion*

See the back of this volume for a complete list of titles in Prometheus's Great Books in Philosophy and Great Minds series.

JOHN STUART MILL was born in London on May 20, 1806, the son of noted Scottish economist and philosopher James Mill, who held an influential post in the powerful East India Company. Mill's natural talent and physical stamina were put to the test at a very young age when he undertook a highly structured and individualized upbringing orchestrated by his father, who believed that the mind was a passive receptacle for human experience. His education and training were so intense that he was reading Greek at the age of three and doing independent writing at six.

Mill's education broadened considerably after 1823 when he entered the East India Company to commence his life's career as his father had done before him. He traveled, became politically involved, and in so doing moved away from the narrower sectarian attitudes in which he had been raised. His ideas and imagination were ignited by the views of such diverse personalities as Wordsworth, Saint-Simon, Coleridge, Comte, and de Tocqueville. During his life, Mill wrote many influential works: *System of Logic* (1843); *Principles of Political Economy* (1848); On *Liberty* (1859); *The Subjection of Women* (1861); *Utilitarianism* (1863); *Examination of Sir William Hamilton's Philosophy* (1865); and *Autobiography* (1873). As a defender of individual freedom and human rights, John Stuart Mill lives on as a nineteenth-century champion of social reform. He died on May 7, 1873.

# CONTENTS

                                         PAGE

NATURE . . . . . . . . . . . . . . . . . 3

UTILITY OF RELIGION . . . . . . . . . . . 69

THEISM . . . . . . . . . . . . . . . . . 125

## PART I

INTRODUCTION . . . . . . . . . . . . . . 125

THEISM . . . . . . . . . . . . . . . . . 130

THE EVIDENCES OF THEISM . . . . . . . . . . 138

ARGUMENT FOR A FIRST CAUSE . . . . . . . . 142

ARGUMENT FROM THE GENERAL CONSENT OF MANKIND . . 155

THE ARGUMENT FROM CONSCIOUSNESS . . . . . . . 161

THE ARGUMENT FROM MARKS OF DESIGN IN NATURE . . . 167

## PART II

ATTRIBUTES . . . . . . . . . . . . . . . 176

## PART III

IMMORTALITY . . . . . . . . . . . . . . . 197

## PART IV

REVELATION . . . . . . . . . . . . . . . 212

## PART V

GENERAL RESULT . . . . . . . . . . . . . . 242

# NATURE

# NATURE

NATURE, natural, and the group of words derived
from them, or allied to them in etymology, have
at all times filled a great place in the thoughts and
taken a strong hold on the feelings of mankind.   That
they should have done so is not surprising, when we
consider what the words, in their primitive and most
obvious signification, represent; but it is unfortunate
that a set of terms which play so great a part in
moral and metaphysical speculation, should have
acquired many meanings different from the primary
one, yet sufficiently allied to it to admit of confusion.
The words have thus become entangled in so many
foreign associations, mostly of a very powerful and
tenacious character, that they have come to excite, and
to be the symbols of, feelings which their original
meaning will by no means justify; and which have
made them one of the most copious sources of false taste,
false philosophy, false morality, and even bad law.

The most important application of the Socratic
Elenchus, as exhibited and improved by Plato, consists
in dissecting large abstractions of this description;
fixing down to a precise definition the meaning which
as popularly used they merely shadow forth, and
questioning and testing the common maxims and
opinions in which they bear a part. It is to be
regretted that among the instructive specimens of this
kind of investigation which Plato has left, and to
which subsequent times have been so much indebted for
whatever intellectual clearness they have attained, he
has not enriched posterity with a dialogue περὶ φύσεως.
If the idea denoted by the word had been subjected
to his searching analysis, and the popular common-
places in which it figures had been submitted to the
ordeal of his powerful dialectics, his successors probably
would not have rushed, as they speedily did, into
modes of thinking and reasoning of which the fallacious use of that word formed the corner stone; a kind
of fallacy from which he was himself singularly free.

According to the Platonic method which is still the
best type of such investigations, the first thing to be
done with so vague a term is to ascertain precisely
what it means. It is also a rule of the same method,
that the meaning of an abstraction is best sought for
in the concrete—of an universal in the particular.
Adopting this course with the word Nature, the first
question must be, what is meant by the "nature" of

a particular object? as of fire, of water, or of some individual plant or animal? Evidently the *ensemble* or aggregate of its powers or properties: the modes in which it acts on other things (counting among those things the senses of the observer) and the modes in which other things act upon it; to which, in the case of a sentient being, must be added, its own capacities of feeling, or being conscious. The Nature of the thing means all this; means its entire capacity of exhibiting phenomena. And since the phenomena which a thing exhibits, however much they vary in different circumstances, are always the same in the same circumstances, they admit of being described in general forms of words, which are called the *laws* of the thing's nature. Thus it is a law of the nature of water that under the mean pressure of the atmosphere at the level of the sea, it boils at 212° Fahrenheit.

As the nature of any given thing is the aggregate of its powers and properties, so Nature in the abstract is the aggregate of the powers and properties of all things. Nature means the sum of all phenomena, together with the causes which produce them; including not only all that happens, but all that is capable of happening; the unused capabilities of causes being as much a part of the idea of Nature, as those which take effect. Since all phenomena which have been sufficiently examined are found to take place with regularity, each having certain fixed conditions, positive and negative, on the occurrence of which it invariably happens ; mankind have been able to ascertain, either by direct observation or by reasoning processes grounded on it, the conditions of the occurrence of many phenomena ; and the progress of science mainly consists in ascertaining those conditions. When discovered they can be expressed in general propositions, which are called laws of the particular phenomenon, and also, more generally, Laws of Nature. Thus, the truth that all material objects tend towards one another with a force directly as their masses and inversely as the square of their distance, is a law of Nature. The proposition that air and food are necessary to animal life, if it be as we have good reason to believe, true without exception, is also a law of nature, though the phenomenon of which it is the law is special, and not, like gravitation, universal.

Nature, then, in this its simplest acceptation, is a collective name for all facts, actual and possible : or (to speak more accurately) a name for the mode, partly known to us and partly unknown, in which all things take place. For the word suggests, not so much the multitudinous detail of the phenomena, as the conception which might be formed of their manner of existence as a mental whole, by a mind possessing a complete knowledge of them : to which conception it is the aim of science to raise itself, by successive steps of generalization from experience.

Such, then, is a correct definition of the word Nature. But this definition corresponds only to one of the senses of that ambiguous term. It is evidently inapplicable to some of the modes in which the word is familiarly employed. For example, it entirely conflicts with the common form of speech by which Nature is opposed to Art, and natural to artificial. For in the sense of the word Nature which has just been defined, and which is the true scientific sense, Art is as much Nature as anything else; and everything which is artificial is natural—Art has no independent powers of its own: Art is but the employment of the powers of Nature for an end. Phenomena produced by human agency, no less than those which as far as we are concerned are spontaneous, depend on the properties of the elementary forces, or of the elementary substances and their compounds. The united powers of the whole human race could not create a new property of matter in general, or of any one of its species. We can only take advantage for our purposes of the properties which we find. A ship floats by the same laws of specific gravity and equilibrium, as a tree uprooted by the wind and blown into the water. The corn which men raise for food, grows and produces its grain by the same laws of vegetation by which the wild rose and the mountain strawberry bring forth their flowers and fruit. A house stands and holds together by the natural properties, the weight and cohesion of the materials which compose it : a steam engine works by the natural expansive force of steam, exerting a pressure upon one part of a system of arrangements, which pressure, by the mechanical properties of the lever, is transferred from that to another part where it raises the weight or removes the obstacle brought into connexion with it. In these and all other artificial operations the office of man is, as has often been remarked, a very limited one ; it consists in moving things into certain places. We move objects, and by doing this, bring some things into contact which were separate, or separate others which were in contact : and by this simple change of place, natural forces previously dormant are called into action, and produce the desired effect. Even the volition which designs, the intelligence which contrives, and the muscular force which executes these movements, are themselves powers of Nature.

It thus appears that we must recognize at least two principal meanings in the word Nature. In one sense, it means all the powers existing in either the outer or the inner world and everything which takes place by means of those powers. In another sense, it means, not everything which happens, but only what takes place without the agency, or without the voluntary and intentional agency, of man. This distinction is far from exhausting the ambiguities of the

word; but it is the key to most of those on which
important consequences depend.

Such, then, being the two principal senses of the
word Nature; in which of these is it taken, or is it
taken in either, when the word and its derivatives are
used to convey ideas of commendation, approval, and
even moral obligation?

It has conveyed such ideas in all ages. *Naturam
sequi* was the fundamental principle of morals in many
of the most admired schools of philosophy. Among
the ancients, especially in the declining period of
ancient intellect and thought, it was the test to which
all ethical doctrines were brought. The Stoics and the
Epicureans, however irreconcilable in the rest of their
systems, agreed in holding themselves bound to prove
that their respective maxims of conduct were the
dictates of nature. Under their influence the Roman
jurists, when attempting to systematize jurisprudence,
placed in the front of their exposition a certain *Jus
Naturale*, "quod natura", as Justinian declares in
the Institutes, "omnia animalia docuit": and as the
modern systematic writers not only on law but on
moral philosophy, have generally taken the Roman
jurists for their models, treatises on the so-called Law
of Nature have abounded; and references to this Law
as a supreme rule and ultimate standard have per-
vaded literature. The writers on International Law
have done more than any others to give currency to

this style of ethical speculation ; inasmuch as having no positive law to write about, and yet being anxious to invest the most approved opinions respecting international morality with as much as they could of the authority of law, they endeavoured to find such an authority in Nature's imaginary code. The Christian theology during the period of its greatest ascendancy, opposed some, though not a complete, hindrance to the modes of thought which erected Nature into the criterion of morals, inasmuch as, according to the creed of most denominations of Christians (though assuredly not of Christ) man is by nature wicked. But this very doctrine, by the reaction which it provoked, has made the deistical moralists almost unanimous in proclaiming the divinity of Nature, and setting up its fancied dictates as an authoritative rule of action. A reference to that supposed standard is the predominant ingredient in the vein of thought and feeling which was opened by Rousseau, and which has infiltrated itself most widely into the modern mind, not excepting that portion of it which calls itself Christian. The doctrines of Christianity have in every age been largely accommodated to the philosophy which happened to be prevalent, and the Christianity of our day has borrowed a considerable part of its colour and flavour from sentimental deism. At the present time it cannot be said that Nature, or any other standard, is applied as it was wont to be, to deduce rules of action with juridical precision, and with an attempt to make its application co-extensive with all human agency. The people of this generation do not commonly apply principles with any such studious exactness, nor own such binding allegiance to any standard, but live in a kind of confusion of many standards; a condition not propitious to the formation of steady moral convictions, but convenient enough to those whose moral opinions sit lightly on them, since it gives them a much wider range of arguments for defending the doctrine of the moment. But though perhaps no one could now be found who like the institutional writers of former times, adopts the so-called Law of Nature as the foundation of ethics, and endeavours consistently to reason from it, the word and its cognates must still be counted among those which carry great weight in moral argumentation. That any mode of thinking, feeling, or acting, is "according to nature" is usually accepted as a strong argument for its goodness. If it can be said with any plausibility that "nature enjoins" anything, the propriety of obeying the injunction is by most people considered to be made out: and conversely, the imputation of being contrary to nature, is thought to bar the door against any pretension on the part of the thing so designated, to be tolerated or excused; and the word unnatural has not ceased to be one of the most vituperative epithets in the language. Those who deal in these expressions, may avoid making themselves responsible for any fundamental theorem respecting the standard of moral obligation, but they do not the less imply such a theorem, and one which must be the same in substance with that on which the more logical thinkers of a more laborious age grounded their systematic treatises on Natural Law.

Is it necessary to recognize in these forms of speech, another distinct meaning of the word Nature? Or can they be connected, by any rational bond of union, with either of the two meanings already treated of? At first it may seem that we have no option but to admit another ambiguity in the term. All inquiries are either into what is, or into what ought to be : science and history belonging to the first division, art, morals and politics to the second. But the two senses of the word Nature first pointed out, agree in referring only to what is. In the first meaning, Nature is a collective name for everything which is. In the second, it is a name for everything which is of itself, without voluntary human intervention. But the employment of the word Nature as a term of ethics seems to disclose a third meaning, in which Nature does not stand for what is, but for what ought to be ; or for the rule or standard of what ought to be. A little consideration, however, will show that this is not a case of ambiguity ; there is not here a third sense of the word. Those who set up Nature as a standard of action do not intend a merely verbal proposition ; they do not mean that the standard, whatever it be, should be *called* Nature ; they think they are giving some information as to what the standard of action really is. Those who say that we ought to act according to Nature do not mean the mere identical proposition that we ought to do what we ought to do. They think that the word Nature affords some external criterion of what we should do ; and if they lay down as a rule for what ought to be, a word which in its proper signification denotes what is, they do so because they have a notion, either clearly or confusedly, that what is, constitutes the rule and standard of what ought to be.

The examination of this notion, is the object of the present Essay. It is proposed to inquire into the truth of the doctrines which make Nature a test of right and wrong, good and evil, or which in any mode or degree attach merit or approval to following, imitating, or obeying Nature. To this inquiry the foregoing discussion respecting the meaning of terms, was an indispensable introduction. Language is as it were the atmosphere of philosophical investigation, which must be made transparent before anything can be seen through it in the true figure and position. In the present case it is necessary to guard against a further ambiguity, which though abundantly obvious, has sometimes misled even sagacious minds, and of which it is well to take distinct note before proceeding further. No word is more commonly associated with the word Nature, than Law; and this last word has distinctly two meanings, in one of which it denotes some definite portion of what is, in the other, of what ought to be. We speak of the law of gravitation, the three laws of motion, the law of definite proportions in chemical combination, the vital laws of organized beings. All these are portions of what is. We also speak of the criminal law, the civil law, the law of honour, the law of veracity, the law of justice; all of which are portions of what ought to be, or of somebody's suppositions, feelings, or commands respecting what ought to be. The first kind of laws, such as the laws of motion, and of gravitation, are neither more nor less than the observed uniformities in the occurrence of phenomena: partly uniformities of antecedence and sequence, partly of concomitance. These are what, in science, and even in ordinary parlance, are meant by laws of nature. Laws in the other sense are the laws of the land, the law of nations, or moral laws; among which, as already noticed, is dragged in, by jurists and publicists, something which they think proper to call the Law of Nature. Of the liability of these two meanings of the word to be confounded there can be no better example than the first chapter of Montesquieu; where he remarks, that the material world has its laws, the inferior animals have their laws, and man has his laws; and calls attention to the much greater strictness with which the first two sets of laws are observed, than the last; as if it were an inconsistency, and a paradox, that things always are what they are, but men not always what they ought to be. A similar confusion of ideas pervades the writings of Mr. George Combe, from whence it has overflowed into a large region of popular literature, and we are now continually reading injunctions to obey the physical laws of the universe, as being obligatory in the same sense and manner as the moral. The conception which the ethical use of the word Nature implies, of a close relation if not absolute identity between what is and what ought to be, certainly derives part of its hold on the mind from the custom of designating what is, by the expression "laws of nature," while the same word Law is also used, and even more familiarly and emphatically, to express what ought to be.

When it is asserted, or implied, that Nature, or the laws of Nature, should be conformed to, is the Nature which is meant, Nature in the first sense of the term, meaning all which is—the powers and properties of all things? But in this signification, there is no need of a recommendation to act according to nature, since it is what nobody can possibly help doing, and equally whether he acts well or ill. There is no mode of acting which is not conformable to Nature in this sense of the term, and all modes of acting are so in exactly the same degree. Every action is the exertion of some natural power, and its effects of all sorts are so many phenomena of nature, produced by the powers and properties of some of the objects of nature, in exact obedience to some law or laws of nature. When I voluntarily use my organs to take in food, the act, and its consequences, take place according to laws of nature : if instead of food I swallow poison, the case is exactly the same. To bid people conform to the laws of nature when they have no power but what the laws of nature give them—when it is a physical im· possibility for them to do the smallest thing otherwise than through some law of nature, is an absurdity. The thing they need to be told is, what particular law of nature they should make use of in a particular case. When, for example, a person is crossing a river by a narrow bridge to which there is no parapet, he will do well to regulate his proceedings by the laws of equilibrium in moving bodies, instead of conforming only to the law of gravitation, and falling into the river.

Yet, idle as it is to exhort people to do what they cannot avoid doing, and absurd as it is to prescribe as a rule of right conduct what agrees exactly as well with wrong; nevertheless a rational rule of conduct *may* be constructed out of the relation which it ought to bear to the laws of nature in this widest acceptation of the term. Man necessarily obeys the laws of nature, or in other words the properties of things, but he does not necessarily *guide* himself by them. Though all conduct is in conformity to laws of nature, all conduct is not grounded on knowledge of them, and intelligently directed to the attainment of purposes by means of them. Though we cannot emancipate ourselves from the laws of nature as a whole, we can escape from any particular law of nature, if we are able to withdraw ourselves from the circumstances in which it acts. Though we can do nothing except through laws of nature, we can use one law to counteract another. According to Bacon's maxim, we can obey nature in such a manner as to command it. Every alteration of circumstances alters more or less the laws of nature under which we act; and by every choice which we make either of ends or of means, we place ourselves to a greater or less extent under one set of laws of nature instead of another. If, therefore, the useless precept to follow nature were changed into a precept to study nature; to know and take heed of the properties of the things we have to deal with, so far as these properties are capable of forwarding or obstructing any given purpose; we should have arrived at the first principle of all intelligent action, or rather at the definition of intelligent action itself. And a confused notion of this true principle, is, I doubt not, in the minds of many of those who set up the unmeaning doctrine which superficially resembles it.

They perceive that the essential difference between wise and foolish conduct consists in attending, or not attending, to the particular laws of nature on which some important result depends.  And they think, that a person who attends to a law of nature in order to shape his conduct by it, may be said to obey it, while a person who practically disregards it, and acts as if no such law existed, may be said to disobey it : the circumstance being overlooked, that what is thus called disobedience to a law of nature is obedience to some other or perhaps to the very law itself.  For example, a person who goes into a powder magazine either not knowing, or carelessly omitting to think of, the explosive force of gunpowder, is likely to do some act which will cause him to be blown to atoms in obedience to the very law which he has disregarded.

But however much of its authority the "Naturam sequi" doctrine may owe to its being confounded with the rational precept "Naturam observare," its favourers and promoters unquestionably intend much more by it than that precept.  To acquire knowledge of the properties of things, and make use of the knowledge for guidance, is a rule of prudence, for the adaptation of means to ends; for giving effect to our wishes and intentions whatever they may be.  But the maxim of obedience to Nature, or conformity to Nature, is held up not as a simply prudential but as an ethical maxim ; and by those who talk of *jus naturæ*, even as a law, fit to be administered by tribunals and enforced by sanctions. Right action, must mean something more and other than merely intelligent action : yet no precept beyond this last, can be connected with the word Nature in the wider and more philosophical of its acceptations. We must try it therefore in the other sense, that in which Nature stands distinguished from Art, and denotes, not the whole course of the pheno- mena which come under our observation, but only their spontaneous course.

Let us then consider whether we can attach any meaning to the supposed practical maxim of following Nature, in this second sense of the word, in which Nature stands for that which takes place without hu- man intervention. In Nature as thus understood, is the spontaneous course of things when left to them- selves, the rule to be followed in endeavouring to adapt things to our use? But it is evident at once that the maxim, taken in this sense, is not merely, as it is in the other sense, superfluous and unmeaning, but palpably absurd and self-contradictory. For while human action cannot help conforming to Nature in the one meaning of the term, the very aim and ob- ject of action is to alter and improve Nature in the other meaning. If the natural course of things were perfectly right and satisfactory, to act at all would be a gratuitous meddling, which as it could not make things better, must make them worse. Or if action at

all could be justified, it would only be when in direct
obedience to instincts, since these might perhaps be
accounted part of the spontaneous order of Nature ;
but to do anything with forethought and purpose,
would be a violation of that perfect order.  If the
artificial is not better than the natural, to what end are
all the arts of life ?  To dig, to plough, to build, to
wear clothes, are direct infringements of the injunction to follow nature.

Accordingly it would be said by every one, even of
those most under the influence of the feelings which
prompt the injunction, that to apply it to such cases
as those just spoken of, would be to push it too far.
Everybody professes to approve and admire many
great triumphs of Art over Nature : the junction by
bridges of shores which Nature had made separate,
the draining of Nature's marshes, the excavation of
her wells, the dragging to light of what she has
buried at immense depths in the earth ; the turning
away of her thunderbolts by lightning rods, of her
inundations by embankments, of her ocean by break-
waters.   But to commend these and similar feats, is
to acknowledge that the ways of Nature are to be
conquered, not obeyed : that her powers are often
towards man in the position of enemies, from whom
he must wrest, by force and ingenuity, what little
he can for his own use, and deserves to be applauded
when that little is rather more than might be ex-

pected from his physical weakness in comparison to those gigantic powers. All praise of Civilization, or Art, or Contrivance, is so much dispraise of Nature; an admission of imperfection, which it is man's business, and merit, to be always endeavouring to correct or mitigate.

The consciousness that whatever man does to improve his condition is in so much a censure and a thwarting of the spontaneous order of Nature, has in all ages caused new and unprecedented attempts at improvement to be generally at first under a shade of religious suspicion; as being in any case uncomplimentary, and very probably offensive to the powerful beings (or, when polytheism gave place to monotheism, to the all-powerful Being) supposed to govern the various phenomena of the universe, and of whose will the course of nature was conceived to be the expression. Any attempt to mould natural phenomena to the convenience of mankind might easily appear an interference with the government of those superior beings : and though life could not have been maintained, much less made pleasant, without perpetual interferences of the kind, each new one was doubtless made with fear and trembling, until experience had shown that it could be ventured on without drawing down the vengeance of the Gods. The sagacity of priests showed them a way to reconcile the impunity of particular infringements with the maintenance of the general dread of encroaching on the divine administration. This was effected by representing each of the principal human inventions as the gift and favour of some God. The old religions also afforded many resources for consulting the Gods, and obtaining their express permission for what would otherwise have appeared a breach of their prerogative. When oracles had ceased, any religion which recognized a revelation afforded expedients for the same purpose. The Catholic religion had the resource of an infallible Church, authorized to declare what exertions of human spontaneity were permitted or forbidden; and in default of this, the case was always open to argument from the Bible whether any particular practice had expressly or by implication been sanctioned. The notion remained that this liberty to control Nature was conceded to man only by special indulgence, and as far as required by his necessities; and there was always a tendency, though a diminishing one, to regard any attempt to exercise power over nature, beyond a certain degree, and a certain admitted range, as an impious effort to usurp divine power, and dare more than was permitted to man. The lines of Horace in which the familiar arts of shipbuilding and navigation are reprobated as *vetitum nefas*, indicate even in that sceptical age a still unexhausted vein of the old sentiment. The intensity of the corresponding feeling in the middle ages is not a precise parallel, on account of the superstition about dealing with evil spirits with which it was complicated: but the imputation of prying into the secrets of the Almighty long remained a powerful weapon of attack against unpopular inquirers into nature; and the charge of presumptuously attempting to defeat the designs of Providence, still retains enough of its original force to be thrown in as a make-weight along with other objections when there is a desire to find fault with any new exertion of human forethought and contrivance. No one, indeed, asserts it to be the intention of the Creator that the spontaneous order of the creation should not be altered, or even that it should not be altered in any new way. But there still exists a vague notion that though it is very proper to control this or the other natural phenomenon, the general scheme of nature is a model for us to imitate: that with more or less liberty in details, we should on the whole be guided by the spirit and general conception of nature's own ways: that they are God's work, and as such perfect; that man cannot rival their unapproachable excellence, and can best show his skill and piety by attempting, in however imperfect a way, to reproduce their likeness; and that if not the whole, yet some particular parts of the spontaneous order of nature, selected according to the speaker's predilections, are in a peculiar sense, manifestations of the Creator's

will; a sort of finger posts pointing out the direction
which things in general, and therefore our voluntary
actions, are intended to take. Feelings of this sort,
though repressed on ordinary occasions by the
contrary current of life, are ready to break out
whenever custom is silent, and the native promptings
of the mind have nothing opposed to them but
reason : and appeals are continually made to them by
rhetoricians, with the effect, if not of convincing
opponents, at least of making those who already hold
the opinion which the rhetorician desires to recommend, better satisfied with it. For in the present
day it probably seldom happens that any one is
persuaded to approve any course of action because it
appears to him to bear an analogy to the divine
government of the world, though the argument tells
on him with great force, and is felt by him to be a
great support, in behalf of anything which he is
already inclined to approve.

If this notion of imitating the ways of Providence
as manifested in Nature, is seldom expressed plainly
and downrightly as a maxim of general application, it
also is seldom directly contradicted. Those who find it
on their path, prefer to turn the obstacle rather than
to attack it, being often themselves not free from the
feeling, and in any case afraid of incurring the charge
of impiety by saying anything which might be held
to disparage the works of the Creator's power. They

therefore, for the most part, rather endeavour to show, that they have as much right to the religious argument as their opponents, and that if the course they recommend seems to conflict with some part of the ways of Providence, there is some other part with which it agrees better than what is contended for on the other side.   In this mode of dealing with the great *à priori* fallacies, the progress of improvement clears away particular errors while the causes of errors are still left standing, and very little weakened by each conflict : yet by a long series of such partial victories precedents are accumulated, to which an appeal may be made against these powerful prepossessions, and which afford a growing hope that the misplaced feeling, after having so often learnt to recede, may some day be compelled to an unconditional surrender.   For however offensive the proposition may appear to many religious persons, they should be willing to look in the face the undeniable fact, that the order of nature, in so far as unmodified by man, is such as no being, whose attributes are justice and benevolence, would have made, with the intention that his rational creatures should follow it as an example.   If made wholly by such a Being, and not partly by beings of very different qualities, it could only be as a designedly imperfect work, which man, in his limited sphere, is to exercise justice and benevolence in amending.   The best persons have always held it to be the essence of religion, that the paramount duty of man upon earth is to amend himself : but all except monkish quietists have annexed to this in their inmost minds (though seldom willing to enunciate the obligation with the same clearness) the additional religious duty of amending the world, and not solely the human part of it but the material; the order of physical nature.

In considering this subject it is necessary to divest ourselves of certain preconceptions which may justly be called natural prejudices, being grounded on feelings which, in themselves natural and inevitable, intrude into matters with which they ought to have no concern. One of these feelings is the astonishment, rising into awe, which is inspired (even independently of all religious sentiment) by any of the greater natural phenomena. A hurricane; a mountain precipice; the desert; the ocean, either agitated or at rest; the solar system, and the great cosmic forces which hold it together; the boundless firmament, and to an educated mind any single star; excite feelings which make all human enterprises and powers appear so insignificant, that to a mind thus occupied it seems insufferable presumption in so puny a creature as man to look critically on things so far above him, or dare to measure himself against the grandeur of the universe. But a little interrogation of our own consciousness will suffice to convince us,

that what makes these phenomena so impressive is
simply their vastness.  The enormous extension in
space  and  time,  or  the  enormous  power  they
exemplify,  constitutes  their  sublimity;  a feeling  in
all  cases,  more  allied  to  terror  than  to  any  moral
emotion.  And though the vast scale of these phenomena may well excite wonder, and sets at defiance all
idea of rivalry, the feeling it inspires is of a totally
different  character  from  admiration  of  excellence.
Those  in  whom  awe  produces  admiration  may  be
æsthetically developed, but they are morally uncultivated.  It is one of the endowments of the imaginative  part  of  our  mental  nature  that  conceptions  of
greatness  and  power,  vividly  realized,  produce  a
feeling  which  though  in  its  higher  degrees  closely
bordering  on  pain,  we  prefer  to  most  of  what  are
accounted  pleasures.  But  we  are  quite  equally
capable  of  experiencing  this  feeling  towards  male-
ficent power; and we never experience it so strongly
towards  most  of  the  powers  of  the  universe,  as  when
we  have  most  present  to  our  consciousness  a  vivid
sense  of  their  capacity  of  inflicting  evil.  Because
these  natural  powers  have  what  we  cannot  imitate,
enormous might, and overawe us by that one attribute,
it  would  be  a  great  error  to  infer  that  their  other
attributes  are  such  as  we  ought  to  emulate,  or  that
we  should  be  justified  in  using  our  small  powers  after
the example which Nature sets us with her vast forces.

For, how stands the fact? That next to the greatness of these cosmic forces, the quality which most forcibly strikes every one who does not avert his eyes from it, is their perfect and absolute recklessness. They go straight to their end, without regarding what or whom they crush on the road. Optimists, in their attempts to prove that "whatever is, is right," are obliged to maintain, not that Nature ever turns one step from her path to avoid trampling us into destruction, but that it would be very unreasonable in us to expect that she should. Pope's "Shall gravitation cease when you go by?" may be a just rebuke to any one who should be so silly as to expect common human morality from nature. But if the question were between two men, instead of between a man and a natural phenomenon, that triumphant apostrophe would be thought a rare piece of impudence. A man who should persist in hurling stones or firing cannon when another man "goes by," and having killed him should urge a similar plea in exculpation, would very deservedly be found guilty of murder.

In sober truth, nearly all the things which men are hanged or imprisoned for doing to one another, are nature's every day performances. Killing, the most criminal act recognized by human laws, Nature does once to every being that lives; and in a large proportion of cases, after protracted tortures such as only

the greatest monsters whom we read of ever purposely
inflicted on their living fellow-creatures. If, by an
arbitrary reservation, we refuse to account anything
murder but what abridges a certain term supposed to
be allotted to human life, nature also does this to all
but a small percentage of lives, and does it in all the
modes, violent or insidious, in which the worst human
beings take the lives of one another. Nature impales
men, breaks them as if on the wheel, casts them to be
devoured by wild beasts, burns them to death, crushes
them with stones like the first christian martyr,
starves them with hunger, freezes them with cold,
poisons them by the quick or slow venom of her ex-
halations, and has hundreds of other hideous deaths
in reserve, such as the ingenious cruelty of a Nabis or
a Domitian never surpassed. All this, Nature does
with the most supercilious disregard both of mercy
and of justice, emptying her shafts upon the best and
noblest indifferently with the meanest and worst ;
upon those who are engaged in the highest and
worthiest enterprises, and often as the direct consequence of the noblest acts ; and it might almost
be imagined as a punishment for them. She mows
down those on whose existence hangs the well-being
of a whole people, perhaps the prospects of the human
race for generations to come, with as little compunc-
tion as those whose death is a relief to themselves, or
a blessing to those under their noxious influence.

Such are Nature's dealings with life. Even when she
does not intend to kill, she inflicts the same tortures
in apparent wantonness. In the clumsy provision
which she has made for that perpetual renewal of
animal life, rendered necessary by the prompt termination she puts to it in every individual instance, no
human being ever comes into the world but another
human being is literally stretched on the rack for
hours or days, not unfrequently issuing in death.
Next to taking life (equal to it according to a high
authority) is taking the means by which we live; and
Nature does this too on the largest scale and with the
most callous indifference. A single hurricane destroys
the hopes of a season; a flight of locusts, or an
inundation, desolates a district; a trifling chemical
change in an edible root, starves a million of people.
The waves of the sea, like banditti seize and appropriate the wealth of the rich and the little all of the
poor with the same accompaniments of stripping,
wounding, and killing as their human antitypes.
Everything in short, which the worst men commit
either against life or property is perpetrated on a
larger scale by natural agents. Nature has Noyades
more fatal than those of Carrier; her explosions of
fire damp are as destructive as human artillery; her
plague and cholera far surpass the poison cups of the
Borgias. Even the love of " order" which is thought
to be a following of the ways of Nature, is in fact

a contradiction of them. All which people are accustomed to deprecate as "disorder" and its consequences, is precisely a counterpart of Nature's ways. Anarchy and the Reign of Terror are overmatched in injustice, ruin, and death, by a hurricane and a pestilence.

But, it is said, all these things are for wise and good ends. On this I must first remark that whether they are so or not, is altogether beside the point. Supposing it true that contrary to appearances these horrors when perpetrated by Nature, promote good ends, still as no one believes that good ends would be promoted by our following the example, the course of Nature cannot be a proper model for us to imitate. Either it is right that we should kill because nature kills; torture because nature tortures; ruin and devastate because nature does the like; or we ought not to consider at all what nature does, but what it is good to do. If there is such a thing as a *reductio ad absurdum*, this surely amounts to one. If it is a sufficient reason for doing one thing, that nature does it, why not another thing? If not all things, why anything? The physical government of the world being full of the things which when done by men are deemed the greatest enormities, it cannot be religious or moral in us to guide our actions by the analogy of the course of nature. This proposition remains true, whatever occult quality of producing good may reside in those facts of nature which to our perceptions are most noxious, and which no one considers it other than a crime to produce artificially.

But, in reality, no one consistently believes in any such occult quality. The phrases which ascribe perfection to the course of nature can only be considered as the exaggerations of poetic or devotional feeling, not intended to stand the test of a sober examination. No one, either religious or irreligious, believes that the hurtful agencies of nature, considered as a whole, promote good purposes, in any other way than by inciting human rational creatures to rise up and struggle against them. If we believed that those agencies were appointed by a benevolent Providence as the means of accomplishing wise purposes which could not be compassed if they did not exist, then everything done by mankind which tends to chain up these natural agencies or to restrict their mischievous operation, from draining a pestilential marsh down to curing the toothache, or putting up an umbrella, ought to be accounted impious; which assuredly nobody does account them, notwithstanding an undercurrent of sentiment setting in that direction which is occasionally perceptible. On the contrary, the improvements on which the civilized part of mankind most pride themselves, consist in more successfully warding off those natural calamities which if we really believed what most people profess

to believe, we should cherish as medicines provided
for our earthly state by infinite wisdom. Inasmuch
too as each generation greatly surpasses its pre-
decessors in the amount of natural evil which it
succeeds in averting, our condition, if the theory
were true, ought by this time to have become a
terrible manifestation of some tremendous calamity,
against which the physical evils we have learnt to
overmaster, had previously operated as a pre-
servative. Any one, however, who acted as if he
supposed this to be the case, would be more likely, I
think, to be confined as a lunatic, than reverenced as
a saint.

It is undoubtedly a very common fact that good
comes out of evil, and when it does occur, it is far
too agreeable not to find people eager to dilate on it.
But in the first place, it is quite as often true of
human crimes, as of natural calamities. The fire of
London, which is believed to have had so salutary an
effect on the healthiness of the city, would have
produced that effect just as much if it had been really
the work of the "furor papisticus" so long com-
memorated on the Monument. The deaths of those
whom tyrants or persecutors have made martyrs in
any noble cause, have done a service to mankind
which would not have been obtained if they had died
by accident or disease. Yet whatever incidental and
unexpected benefits may result from crimes, they are

crimes nevertheless. In the second place, if good frequently comes out of evil, the converse fact, evil coming out of good, is equally common. Every event public or private, which, regretted on its occurrence, was declared providential at a later period on account of some unforeseen good consequence, might be matched by some other event, deemed fortunate at the time, but which proved calamitous or fatal to those whom it appeared to benefit. Such conflicts between the beginning and the end, or between the event and the expectation, are not only as frequent, but as often held up to notice, in the painful cases as in the agreeable ; but there is not the same inclination to generalize on them; or at all events they are not regarded by the moderns (though they were by the ancients) as similarly an indication of the divine purposes : men satisfy themselves with moralizing on the imperfect nature of our foresight, the uncertainty of events, and the vanity of human expectations. The simple fact is, human interests are so complicated, and the effects of any incident whatever so multitudinous, that if it touches mankind at all, its influence on them is, in the great majority of cases, both good and bad. If the greater number of personal misfortunes have their good side, hardly any good fortune ever befel any one which did not give either to the same or to some other person, something to regret: and unhappily there are many misfortunes so overwhelming that their favourable side, if it exist, is entirely overshadowed and made insignificant; while the corresponding statement can seldom be made concerning blessings. The effects too of every cause depend so much on the circumstances which accidentally accompany it, that many cases are sure to occur in which even the total result is markedly opposed to the predominant tendency: and thus not only evil has its good and good its evil side, but good often produces an overbalance of evil and evil an overbalance of good. This, however, is by no means the general tendency of either phenomenon. On the contrary, both good and evil naturally tend to fructify, each in its own kind, good producing good, and evil, evil. It is one of Nature's general rules, and part of her habitual injustice, that "to him that hath shall be given, but from him that hath not, shall be taken even that which he hath." The ordinary and predominant tendency of good is towards more good. Health, strength, wealth, knowledge, virtue, are not only good in themselves but facilitate and promote the acquisition of good, both of the same and of other kinds. The person who can learn easily, is he who already knows much: it is the strong and not the sickly person who can do everything which most conduces to health; those who find it easy to gain money are not the poor but the rich; while health, strength, knowledge, talents, are all means of acquiring riches, and riches are often an indispensable means of acquiring these. Again, *e converso*, whatever may be said of evil turning into good, the general tendency of evil is towards further evil. Bodily illness renders the body more susceptible of disease; it produces incapacity of exertion, sometimes debility of mind, and often the loss of means of subsistence. All severe pain, either bodily or mental, tends to increase the susceptibilities of pain for ever after. Poverty is the parent of a thousand mental and moral evils. What is still worse, to be injured or oppressed, when habitual, lowers the whole tone of the character. One bad action leads to others, both in the agent himself, in the bystanders, and in the sufferers. All bad qualities are strengthened by habit, and all vices and follies tend to spread. Intellectual defects generate moral, and moral, intellectual; and every intellectual or moral defect generates others, and so on without end.

That much applauded class of authors, the writers on natural theology, have, I venture to think, entirely lost their way, and missed the sole line of argument which could have made their speculations acceptable to any one who can perceive when two propositions contradict one another. They have exhausted the resources of sophistry to make it appear that all the suffering in the world exists to prevent greater—that misery exists, for fear lest there should be misery : a thesis which if ever so well maintained, could only avail to explain and justify the works of limited beings, compelled to labour under conditions independent of their own will; but can have no application to a Creator assumed to be omnipotent, who, if he bends to a supposed necessity, himself makes the necessity which he bends to. If the maker of the world *can* all that he will, he wills misery, and there is no escape from the conclusion. The more consistent of those who have deemed themselves qualified to "vindicate the ways of God to man" have endeavoured to avoid the alternative by hardening their hearts, and denying that misery is an evil. The goodness of God, they say, does not consist in willing the happiness of his creatures, but their virtue; and the universe, if not a happy, is a just, universe. But waving the objections to this scheme of ethics, it does not at all get rid of the difficulty. If the Creator of mankind willed that they should all be virtuous, his designs are as completely baffled as if he had willed that they should all be happy : and the order of nature is constructed with even less regard to the requirements of justice than to those of benevolence. If the law of all creation were justice and the Creator omnipotent, then in whatever amount suffering and happiness might be dispensed to the world, each person's share of them would be exactly proportioned to that person's good or evil deeds ; no human being would have a worse lot than another, without worse deserts; accident or favouritism would have no part in such a world, but every human life would be the playing out of a drama constructed like a perfect moral tale. No one is able to blind himself to the fact that the world we live in is totally different from this; insomuch that the necessity of redressing the balance has been deemed one of the strongest arguments for another life after death, which amounts to an admission that the order of things in this life is often an example of injustice, not justice. If it be said that God does not take sufficient account of pleasure and pain to make them the reward or punishment of the good or the wicked, but that virtue is itself the greatest good and vice the greatest evil, then these at least ought to be dispensed to all according to what they have done to deserve them; instead of which, every kind of moral depravity is entailed upon multitudes by the fatality of their birth; through the fault of their parents, of society, or of uncontrollable circumstances, certainly through no fault of their own. Not even on the most distorted and contracted theory of good which ever was framed by religious or philosophical fanaticism, can the government of Nature be made to resemble the work of a being at once good and omnipotent.

The only admissible moral theory of Creation is that the Principle of Good *cannot* at once and altogether subdue the powers of evil, either physical or

moral; could not place mankind in a world free from
the necessity of an incessant struggle with the male-
ficent powers, or make them always victorious in that
struggle, but could and did make them capable of
carrying on the fight with vigour and with progres-
sively increasing success. Of all the religious ex-
planations of the order of nature, this alone is neither
contradictory to itself, nor to the facts for which it
attempts to account. According to it, man's duty
would consist, not in simply taking care of his own
interests by obeying irresistible power, but in standing
forward a not ineffectual auxiliary to a Being of perfect beneficence; a faith which seems much better
adapted for nerving him to exertion than a vague and
inconsistent reliance on an Author of Good who is
supposed to be also the author of evil. And I venture
to assert that such has really been, though often
unconsciously, the faith of all who have drawn strength
and support of any worthy kind from trust in a super-
intending Providence. There is no subject on which
men's practical belief is more incorrectly indicated by
the words they use to express it, than religion. Many
have derived a base confidence from imagining themselves to be favourites of an omnipotent but capricious
and despotic Deity. But those who have been strengthened in goodness by relying on the sympathizing
support of a powerful and good Governor of the world,
have, I am satisfied, never really believed that

Governor to be, in the strict sense of the term, omnipotent. They have always saved his goodness at the
expense of his power. They have believed, perhaps,
that he could, if he willed, remove all the thorns from
their individual path, but not without causing greater
harm to some one else, or frustrating some purpose of
greater importance to the general well-being. They
have believed that he could do any one thing, but not
any combination of things: that his government, like
human government, was a system of adjustments and
compromises; that the world is inevitably imperfect,
contrary to his intention.* And since the exertion
of all his power to make it as little imperfect as possible, leaves it no better than it is, they cannot but
regard that power, though vastly beyond human estimate, yet as in itself not merely finite, but extremely
limited. They are bound, for example, to suppose

---

* This irresistible conviction comes out in the writings of religious
philosophers, in exact proportion to the general clearness of their understanding. It nowhere shines forth so distinctly as in Leibnitz's
famous Théodicée, so strangely mistaken for a system of optimism,
and, as such, satirized by Voltaire on grounds which do not even
touch the author's argument. Leibnitz does not maintain that this
world is the best of all imaginable, but only of all possible worlds;
which, he argues, it cannot but be, inasmuch as God, who is absolute
goodness, has chosen it and not another. In every page of the work he
tacitly assumes an abstract possibility and impossibility, independent of
the divine power: and though his pious feelings make him continue to
designate that power by the word Omnipotence, he so explains that
term as to make it mean, power extending to all that is within the
limits of that abstract possibility.

that the best he could do for his human creatures was to make an immense majority of all who have yet existed, be born (without any fault of their own) Patagonians, or Esquimaux, or something nearly as brutal and degraded, but to give them capacities which by being cultivated for very many centuries in toil and suffering, and after many of the best specimens of the race have sacrificed their lives for the purpose, have at last enabled some chosen portions of the species to grow into something better, capable of being improved in centuries more into something really good, of which hitherto there are only to be found individual instances. It may be possible to believe with Plato that perfect goodness, limited and thwarted in every direction by the intractableness of the material, has done this because it could do no better. But that the same perfectly wise and good Being had absolute power over the material, and made it, by voluntary choice, what it is; to admit this might have been supposed impossible to any one who has the simplest notions of moral good and evil. Nor can any such person, whatever kind of religious phrases he may use, fail to believe, that if Nature and Man are both the works of a Being of perfect goodness, that Being intended Nature as a scheme to be amended, not imitated, by Man.

But even though unable to believe that Nature, as a whole, is a realization of the designs of perfect wisdom and benevolence, men do not willingly renounce the idea that some part of Nature, at least, must be intended as an exemplar, or type; that on some portion or other of the Creator's works, the image of the moral qualities which they are accustomed to ascribe to him, must be impressed; that if not all which is, yet something which is, must not only be a faultless model of what ought to be, but must be intended to be our guide and standard in rectifying the rest. It does not suffice them to believe, that what tends to good is to be imitated and perfected, and what tends to evil is to be corrected : they are anxious for some more definite indication of the Creator's designs; and being persuaded that this must somewhere be met with in his works, undertake the dangerous responsibility of picking and choosing among them in quest of it. A choice which except so far as directed by the general maxim that he intends all the good and none of the evil, must of necessity be perfectly arbitrary; and if it leads to any conclusions other than such as can be deduced from that maxim, must be, exactly in that proportion, pernicious.

It has never been settled by any accredited doctrine, what particular departments of the order of nature shall be reputed to be designed for our moral instruction and guidance; and accordingly each person's individual predilections, or momentary convenience, have decided to what parts of the divine government the practical conclusions that he was desirous of establishing, should be recommended to approval as being analogous. One such recommendation must be as fallacious as another, for it is impossible to decide that certain of the Creator's works are more truly expressions of his character than the rest ; and the only selection which does not lead to immoral results, is the selection of those which most conduce to the general good, in other words, of those which point to an end which if the entire scheme is the expression of a single omnipotent and consistent will, is evidently not the end intended by it.

There is however one particular element in the construction of the world, which to minds on the look-out for special indication of the Creator's will, has appeared, not without plausibility, peculiarly fitted to afford them ; viz. the active impulses of human and other animated beings. One can imagine such persons arguing that when the Author of Nature only made circumstances, he may not have meant to indicate the manner in which his rational creatures were to adjust themselves to those circumstances ; but that when he implanted positive stimuli in the creatures themselves, stirring them up to a particular kind of action, it is impossible to doubt that he intended that sort of action to be practised by them. This reasoning, fol-lowed out consistently, would lead to the conclusion that the Deity intended, and approves, whatever human beings do; since all that they do being the consequence of some of the impulses with which their Creator must have endowed them, all must equally be considered as done in obedience to his will. As this practical conclusion was shrunk from, it was necessary to draw a distinction, and to pronounce that not the whole, but only parts of the active nature of mankind point to a special intention of the Creator in respect to their conduct. These parts it seemed natural to suppose, must be those in which the Creator's hand is manifested rather than the man's own: and hence the frequent antithesis between man as God made him, and man as he has made himself. Since what is done with deliberation seems more the man's own act, and he is held more completely responsible for it than for what he does from sudden impulse, the considerate part of human conduct is apt to be set down as man's share in the business, and the inconsiderate as God's. The result is the vein of sentiment so common in the modern world (though unknown to the philosophic ancients) which exalts instinct at the expense of reason; an aberration rendered still more mischievous by the opinion commonly held in conjunction with it, that every, or almost every, feeling or impulse which acts promptly without waiting to ask questions, is an instinct. Thus almost every variety of unreflecting and uncalculating impulse receives a kind of consecration, except those which,

though unreflecting at the moment, owe their origin
to previous habits of reflection : these, being evidently
not instinctive, do not meet with the favour accorded
to the rest; so that all unreflecting impulses are
invested with authority over reason, except the only
ones which are most probably right.  I do not mean,
of course, that this mode of judgment is even pretended to be consistently carried out : life could not
go on if it were not admitted that impulses must be
controlled, and that reason ought to govern our actions.
The pretension is not to drive Reason from the helm
but rather to bind her by articles to steer only in a
particular way.  Instinct is not to govern, but reason
is to practise some vague and unassignable amount of
deference to Instinct.  Though the impression in
favour of instinct as being a peculiar manifestation of
the divine purposes, has not been cast into the form
of a consistent general theory, it remains a standing
prejudice, capable of being stirred up into hostility to
reason in any case in which the dictate of the rational
faculty has not acquired the authority of prescription.

I shall not here enter into the difficult psychological
question, what are, or are not instincts : the subject
would require a volume to itself.  Without touching
upon any disputed theoretical points, it is possible to
judge how little worthy is the instinctive part of human
nature to be held up as its chief excellence—as the part
in which the hand of infinite goodness and wisdom is

peculiarly visible. Allowing everything to be an instinct which anybody has ever asserted to be one, it remains true that nearly every respectable attribute of humanity is the result not of instinct, but of a victory over instinct; and that there is hardly anything valuable in the natural man except capacities—a whole world of possibilities, all of them dependent upon eminently artificial discipline for being realized.

It is only in a highly artificialized condition of human nature that the notion grew up, or, I believe, ever could have grown up, that goodness was natural : because only after a long course of artificial education did good sentiments become so habitual, and so predominant over bad, as to arise unprompted when occasion called for them. In the times when mankind were nearer to their natural state, cultivated observers regarded the natural man as a sort of wild animal, distinguished chiefly by being craftier than the other beasts of the field ; and all worth of character was deemed the result of a sort of taming; a phrase often applied by the ancient philosophers to the appropriate discipline of human beings. The truth is that there is hardly a single point of excellence belonging to human character, which is not decidedly repugnant to the untutored feelings of human nature.

If there be a virtue which more than any other we expect to find, and really do find, in an uncivilized

state, it is the virtue of courage. Yet this is from
first to last a victory achieved over one of the most
powerful emotions of human nature. If there is any
one feeling or attribute more natural than all others to
human beings, it is fear; and no greater proof can be
given of the power of artificial discipline than the
conquest which it has at all times and places shown
itself capable of achieving over so mighty and so
universal a sentiment. The widest difference no doubt
exists between one human being and another in the
facility or difficulty with which they acquire this
virtue. There is hardly any department of human
excellence in which difference of original temperament
goes so far. But it may fairly be questioned if any
human being is naturally courageous. Many are naturally pugnacious, or irascible, or enthusiastic, and these
passions when strongly excited may render them insensible to fear. But take away the conflicting
emotion, and fear reasserts its dominion : consistent
courage is always the effect of cultivation. The
courage which is occasionally though by no means
generally found among tribes of savages, is as much
the result of education as that of the Spartans or
Romans. In all such tribes there is a most emphatic
direction of the public sentiment into every channel
of expression through which honour can be paid to
courage and cowardice held up to contempt and de-
rision. It will perhaps be said, that as the expression

of a sentiment implies the sentiment itself, the training of the young to courage presupposes an originally
courageous people. It presupposes only what all good
customs presuppose—that there must have been individuals better than the rest, who set the customs
going. Some individuals, who like other people had
fears to conquer, must have had strength of mind
and will to conquer them for themselves. These would
obtain the influence belonging to heroes, for that which
is at once astonishing and obviously useful never fails
to be admired: and partly through this admiration,
partly through the fear they themselves excite, they
would obtain the power of legislators, and could
establish whatever customs they pleased.

Let us next consider a quality which forms the most
visible, and one of the most radical of the moral dis-
tinctions between human beings and most of the lower
animals; that of which the absence, more than of
anything else, renders men bestial; the quality of
cleanliness. Can anything be more entirely artificial?
Children, and the lower classes of most countries,
seem to be actually fond of dirt: the vast majority of
the human race are indifferent to it: whole nations
of otherwise civilized and cultivated human beings
tolerate it in some of its worst forms, and only a very
small minority are consistently offended by it. Indeed
the universal law of the subject appears to be, that un-
cleanliness offends only those to whom it is unfamiliar,

so that those who have lived in so artificial a state as
to be unused to it in any form, are the sole persons
whom it disgusts in all forms. Of all virtues this is
the most evidently not instinctive, but a triumph over
instinct. Assuredly neither cleanliness nor the love
of cleanliness is natural to man, but only the capacity
of acquiring a love of cleanliness.

Our examples have thus far been taken from the
personal, or as they are called by Bentham, the self
regarding virtues, because these, if any, might be supposed to be congenial even to the uncultivated mind.
Of the social virtues it is almost superfluous to speak ;
so completely is it the verdict of all experience that
selfishness is natural. By this I do not in any wise mean
to deny that sympathy is natural also; I believe on
the contrary that on that important fact rests the
possibility of any cultivation of goodness and noble-
ness, and the hope of their ultimate entire ascendancy.
But sympathetic characters, left uncultivated, and
given up to their sympathetic instincts, are as selfish
as others. The difference is in the *kind* of selfishness :
theirs is not solitary but sympathetic selfishness ;
*l'egoïsme à deux, à trois*, or *à quatre ;* and they may
be very amiable and delightful to those with whom
they sympathize, and grossly unjust and unfeeling to
the rest of the world. Indeed the finer nervous orga-
nizations which are most capable of and most require
sympathy, have, from their fineness, so much stronger

impulses of all sorts, that they often furnish the most striking examples of selfishness, though of a less repulsive kind than that of colder natures. Whether there ever was a person in whom, apart from all teaching of instructors, friends or books, and from all intentional self-modelling according to an ideal, natural benevolence was a more powerful attribute than selfishness in any of its forms, may remain undecided. That such cases are extremely rare, every one must admit, and this is enough for the argument.

But (to speak no further of self-control for the benefit of others) the commonest self-control for one's own benefit—that power of sacrificing a present desire to a distant object or a general purpose which is indispensable for making the actions of the individual accord with his own notions of his individual good; even this is most unnatural to the undisciplined human being: as may be seen by the long apprenticeship which children serve to it; the very imperfect manner in which it is acquired by persons born to power, whose will is seldom resisted, and by all who have been early and much indulged; and the marked absence of the quality in savages, in soldiers and sailors, and in a somewhat less degree in nearly the whole of the poorer classes in this and many other countries. The principal difference, on the point under consideration, between this virtue and others, is that although, like them, it requires a course of teaching, it is more susceptible than most of them of being self-taught. The axiom is trite that self-control is only learnt by experience: and this endowment is only thus much nearer to being natural than the others we have spoken of, inasmuch as personal experience, without external inculcation, has a certain tendency to engender it. Nature does not of herself bestow this, any more than other virtues; but nature often administers the rewards and punishments which cultivate it, and which in other cases have to be created artificially for the express purpose.

Veracity might seem, of all virtues, to have the most plausible claim to being natural, since in the absence of motives to the contrary, speech usually conforms to, or at least does not intentionally deviate from, fact. Accordingly this is the virtue with which writers like Rousseau delight in decorating savage life, and setting it in advantageous contrast with the treachery and trickery of civilization. Unfortunately this is a mere fancy picture, contradicted by all the realities of savage life. Savages are always liars. They have not the faintest notion of truth as a virtue. They have a notion of not betraying to their hurt, as of not hurting in any other way, persons to whom they are bound by some special tie of obligation; their chief, their guest, perhaps, or their friend: these feelings of obligation being the taught morality of the savage state, growing out of its characteristic circumstances. But of any point of honour respecting truth for truth's sake, they have not the remotest idea ; no more than the whole East, and the greater part of Europe : and in the few countries which are sufficiently improved to have such a point of honour, it is confined to a small minority, who alone, under any circumstances of real temptation practise it.

From the general use of the expression " natural justice," it must be presumed that justice is a virtue generally thought to be directly implanted by nature. I believe, however, that the sentiment of justice is entirely of artificial origin ; the idea of natural justice not preceding but following that of conventional justice. The farther we look back into the early modes of thinking of the human race, whether we consider ancient times (including those of the Old Testament) or the portions of mankind who are still in no more advanced a condition than that of ancient times, the more completely do we find men's notions of justice defined and bounded by the express appointment of law. A man's just rights, meant the rights which the law gave him : a just man, was he who never infringed, nor sought to infringe, the legal property or other legal rights of others. The notion of a higher justice, to which laws themselves are amenable, and by which the conscience is bound without a positive prescription of law, is a later extension of the idea, suggested by, and following the analogy

of, legal justice, to which it maintains a parallel
direction through all the shades and varieties of the
sentiment, and from which it borrows nearly the
whole of its phraseology. The very words *justus* and
*justitia* are derived from *jus*, law. Courts of justice,
administration of justice, always mean the tribunals.

If it be said, that there must be the germs of all these
virtues in human nature, otherwise mankind would
be incapable of acquiring them, I am ready, with a
certain amount of explanation, to admit the fact.
But the weeds that dispute the ground with these
beneficent germs, are themselves not germs but rankly
luxuriant growths, and would, in all but some one
case in a thousand, entirely stifle and destroy the
former, were it not so strongly the interest of mankind to cherish the good germs in one another, that
they always do so, in as far as their degree of intelligence
(in this as in other respects still very imperfect) allows.
It is through such fostering, commenced early, and
not counteracted by unfavourable influences, that, in
some happily circumstanced specimens of the human
race, the most elevated sentiments of which humanity
is capable become a second nature, stronger than the
first, and not so much subduing the original nature as
merging it into itself. Even those gifted organiza-
tions which have attained the like excellence by self-
culture, owe it essentially to the same cause; for
what self-culture would be possible without aid from

the general sentiment of mankind delivered through books, and from the contemplation of exalted characters real or ideal? This artificially created or at least artificially perfected nature of the best and noblest human beings, is the only nature which it is ever commendable to follow. It is almost superfluous to say that even this cannot be erected into a standard of conduct, since it is itself the fruit of a training and culture the choice of which, if rational and not accidental, must have been determined by a standard already chosen.

This brief survey is amply sufficient to prove that the duty of man is the same in respect to his own nature as in respect to the nature of all other things, namely not to follow but to amend it. Some people however who do not attempt to deny that instinct ought to be subordinate to reason, pay deference to nature so far as to maintain that every natural inclination must have some sphere of action granted to it, some opening left for its gratification. All natural wishes, they say, must have been implanted for a purpose: and this argument is carried so far, that we often hear it maintained that every wish, which it is supposed to be natural to entertain, must have a corresponding provision in the order of the universe for its gratification : insomuch (for instance) that the desire of an indefinite prolongation of existence, is believed by many to be in itself a sufficient proof of the reality of a future life.

I conceive that there is a radical absurdity in all these attempts to discover, in detail, what are the designs of Providence, in order when they are discovered to help Providence in bringing them about. Those who argue, from particular indications, that Providence intends this or that, either believe that the Creator can do all that he will or that he cannot. If the first supposition is adopted—if Providence is omnipotent, Providence intends whatever happens, and the fact of its happening proves that Providence intended it. If so, everything which a human being can do, is predestined by Providence and is a fulfilment of its designs. But if as is the more religious theory, Providence intends not all which happens, but only what is good, then indeed man has it in his power, by his voluntary actions, to aid the intentions of Providence; but he can only learn those intentions by considering what tends to promote the general good, and not what man has a natural inclination to ; for, limited as, on this showing, the divine power must be, by inscrutable but insurmountable obstacles, who knows that man *could* have been created without desires which never are to be, and even which never ought to be, fulfilled? The inclinations with which man has been endowed, as well as any of the other contrivances which we observe in Nature, may be the expression not of the divine will, but of the fetters which impede its free action; and to take hints from these for the guidance of our own conduct may be falling into a trap laid by the enemy. The assump tion that everything which infinite goodness can desire, actually comes to pass in this universe, or at least that we must never say or suppose that it does not, is worthy only of those whose slavish fears make them offer the homage of lies to a Being who, they profess to think, is incapable of being deceived and holds all falsehood in abomination.

With regard to this particular hypothesis, that all natural impulses, all propensities sufficiently universal and sufficiently spontaneous to be capable of passing for instincts, must exist for good ends, and ought to be only regulated, not repressed; this is of course true of the majority of them, for the species could not have continued to exist unless most of its inclinations had been directed to things needful or useful for its preservation. But unless the instincts can be reduced to a very small number indeed, it must be allowed that we have also bad instincts which it should be the aim of education not simply to regulate but to extirpate, or rather (what can be done even to an instinct) to starve them by disuse. Those who are inclined to multiply the number of instincts, usually include among them one which they call destructive- ness : an instinct to destroy for destruction's sake. I can conceive no good reason for preserving this, no more than another propensity which if not an instinct

is very like one, what has been called the instinct of
domination; a delight in exercising despotism, in
holding other beings in subjection to our will. The
man who takes pleasure in the mere exertion of
authority, apart from the purpose for which it is to
be employed, is the last person in whose hands one
would willingly entrust it. Again, there are persons
who are cruel by character, or, as the phrase is,
naturally cruel; who have a real pleasure in inflicting,
or seeing the infliction of pain. This kind of cruelty
is not mere hardheartedness, absence of pity or re-
morse; it is a positive thing; a particular kind of
voluptuous excitement. The East, and Southern
Europe, have afforded, and probably still afford,
abundant examples of this hateful propensity. I suppose it will be granted that this is not one of the natural
inclinations which it would be wrong to suppress.
The only question would be whether it is not a duty
to suppress the man himself along with it.

But even if it were true that every one of the
elementary impulses of human nature has its good side,
and may by a sufficient amount of artificial training
be made more useful than hurtful; how little would
this amount to, when it must in any case be admitted
that without such training all of them, even those
which are necessary to our preservation, would fill the
world with misery, making human life an exaggerated
likeness of the odious scene of violence and tyranny

which is exhibited by the rest of the animal kingdom, except in so far as tamed and disciplined by man. There, indeed, those who flatter themselves with the notion of reading the purposes of the Creator in his works, ought in consistency to have seen grounds for inferences from which they have shrunk. If there are any marks at all of special design in creation, one of the things most evidently designed is that a large proportion of all animals should pass their existence in tormenting and devouring other animals. They have been lavishly fitted out with the instruments necessary for that purpose; their strongest instincts impel them to it, and many of them seem to have been constructed incapable of supporting themselves by any other food. If a tenth part of the pains which have been expended in finding benevolent adaptations in all nature, had been employed in collecting evidence to blacken the character of the Creator, what scope for comment would not have been found in the entire existence of the lower animals, divided, with scarcely an exception, into devourers and devoured, and a prey to a thousand ills from which they are denied the faculties necessary for protecting themselves! If we are not obliged to believe the animal creation to be the work of a demon, it is because we need not suppose it to have been made by a Being of infinite power. But if imitation of the Creator's will as revealed in nature, were applied as a rule of action in

this case, the most atrocious enormities of the worst
men would be more than justified by the apparent
intention of Providence that throughout all animated
nature the strong should prey upon the weak.

The preceding observations are far from having
exhausted the almost infinite variety of modes and
occasions in which the idea of conformity to nature
is introduced as an element into the ethical appreciation of actions and dispositions. The same favourable prejudgment follows the word nature through
the numerous acceptations, in which it is employed as
a distinctive term for certain parts of the constitution
of humanity as contrasted with other parts. We
have hitherto confined ourselves to one of these acceptations, in which it stands as a general designation for
those parts of our mental and moral constitution which
are supposed to be innate, in contradistinction to those
which are acquired; as when nature is contrasted with
education; or when a savage state, without laws, arts,
or knowledge, is called a state of nature; or when the
question is asked whether benevolence, or the moral
sentiment, is natural or acquired; or whether some
persons are poets or orators by nature and others not.
But in another and a more lax sense, any manifestations by human beings are often termed natural, when
it is merely intended to say that they are not studied
or designedly assumed in the particular case; as when
a person is said to move or speak with natural grace;

or when it is said that a person's natural manner or
character is so and so ; meaning that it is so when he
does not attempt to control or disguise it.  In a still
looser acceptation, a person is said to be naturally,
that which he was until some special cause had acted
upon him, or which it is supposed he would be if some
such cause were withdrawn.  Thus a person is said
to be naturally dull, but to have made himself intelligent by study and perseverance ; to be naturally
cheerful, but soured by misfortune ; naturally ambi-
tious, but kept down by want of opportunity.  Finally,
the word natural, applied to feelings or conduct, often
seems to mean no more than that they are such as are
ordinarily found in human beings ; as when it is said
that a person acted, on some particular occasion, as it
was natural to do ; or that to be affected in a particular way by some sight, or sound, or thought, or
incident in life, is perfectly natural.

In all these senses of the term, the quality called natural is very often confessedly a worse quality than the
one contrasted with it ; but whenever its being so is
not too obvious to be questioned, the idea seems to be
entertained that by describing it as natural, something
has been said amounting to a considerable presumption in its favour.  For my part I can perceive only
one sense in which nature, or naturalness, in a human
being, are really terms of praise ; and then the praise
is only negative : namely when used to denote the

absence of affectation. Affectation may be defined, the effort to appear what one is not, when the motive or the occasion is not such as either to excuse the attempt, or to stamp it with the more odious name of hypocrisy. It must be added that the deception is often attempted to be practised on the deceiver himself as well as on others; he imitates the external signs of qualities which he would like to have, in hopes to persuade himself that he has them. Whether in the form of deception or of self-deception, or of something hovering between the two, affectation is very rightly accounted a reproach, and naturalness, understood as the reverse of affectation, a merit. But a more proper term by which to express this estimable quality would be sincerity; a term which has fallen from its original elevated meaning, and popularly denotes only a subordinate branch of the cardinal virtue it once designated as a whole.

Sometimes also, in cases where the term affectation would be inappropriate, since the conduct or demeanour spoken of is really praiseworthy, people say in disparagement of the person concerned, that such conduct or demeanour is not natural to him; and make uncomplimentary comparisons between him and some other person, to whom it is natural: meaning that what in the one seemed excellent was the effect of temporary excitement, or of a great victory over himself, while in the other it is the result to be expected from the habitual character. This mode of speech is not open to censure, since nature is here simply a term for the person's ordinary disposition, and if he is praised it is not for being natural, but for being naturally good.

Conformity to nature, has no connection whatever with right and wrong. The idea can never be fitly introduced into ethical discussions at all, except, occasionally and partially, into the question of degrees of culpability. To illustrate this point, let us consider the phrase by which the greatest intensity of condemnatory feeling is conveyed in connection with the idea of nature—the word unnatural. That a thing is unnatural, in any precise meaning which can be attached to the word, is no argument for its being blamable; since the most criminal actions are to a being like man, not more unnatural than most of the virtues. The acquisition of virtue has in all ages been accounted a work of labour and difficulty, while the *dëscensus Averni* on the contrary is of proverbial facility: and it assuredly requires in most persons a greater conquest over a greater number of natural inclinations to become eminently virtuous than transcendently vicious. But if an action, or an inclination, has been decided on other grounds to be blamable, it may be a circumstance in aggravation that it is unnatural, that is, repugnant to some strong feeling usually found in human beings; since the bad propensity, whatever it be, has afforded evidence of being both strong and deeply rooted, by having overcome that repugnance. This presumption of course fails if the individual never had the repugnance : and the argument, therefore, is not fit to be urged unless the feeling which is violated by the act, is not only justifiable and reasonable, but is one which it is blamable to be without.

The corresponding plea in extenuation of a culpable act because it was natural, or because it was prompted by a natural feeling, never, I think, ought to be admitted. There is hardly a bad action ever perpetrated which is not perfectly natural, and the motives to which are not perfectly natural feelings. In the eye of reason, therefore, this is no excuse, but it is quite " natural " that it should be so in the eyes of the multitude ; because the meaning of the expression is, that they have a fellow feeling with the offender. When they say that something which they cannot help admitting to be blamable, is nevertheless natural, they mean that they can imagine the possibility of their being themselves tempted to commit it. Most people have a considerable amount of indulgence towards all acts of which they feel a possible source within themselves, reserving their rigour for those which, though perhaps really less bad, they cannot in any way understand how it is possible to commit. If an action convinces them (which it oftens does on very inadequate grounds) that the person who does it must be a being totally unlike themselves, they are seldom particular in examining the precise degree of blame due to it, or even if blame is properly due to it at all. They measure the degree of guilt by the strength of their antipathy; and hence differences of opinion, and even differences of taste, have been objects of as intense moral abhorrence as the most atrocious crimes.

It will be useful to sum up in a few words the leading conclusions of this Essay.

The word Nature has two principal meanings: it either denotes the entire system of things, with the aggregate of all their properties, or it denotes things as they would be, apart from human intervention.

In the first of these senses, the doctrine that man ought to follow nature is unmeaning; since man has no power to do anything else than follow nature; all his actions are done through, and in obedience to, some one or many of nature's physical or mental laws.

In the other sense of the term, the doctrine that man ought to follow nature, or in other words, ought to make the spontaneous course of things the model of his voluntary actions, is equally irrational and immoral.

Irrational, because all human action whatever, consists in altering, and all useful action in improving, the spontaneous course of nature:

Immoral, because the course of natural phenomena being replete with everything which when committed by human beings is most worthy of abhorrence, any one who endeavoured in his actions to imitate the natural course of things would be universally seen and acknowledged to be the wickedest of men.

The scheme of Nature regarded in its whole extent, cannot have had, for its sole or even principal object, the good of human or other sentient beings. What good it brings to them, is mostly the result of their own exertions. Whatsoever, in nature, gives indication of beneficent design, proves this beneficence to be armed only with limited power; and the duty of man is to co-operate with the beneficent powers, not by imitating but by perpetually striving to amend the course of nature—and bringing that part of it over which we can exercise control, more nearly into conformity with a high standard of justice and goodness.

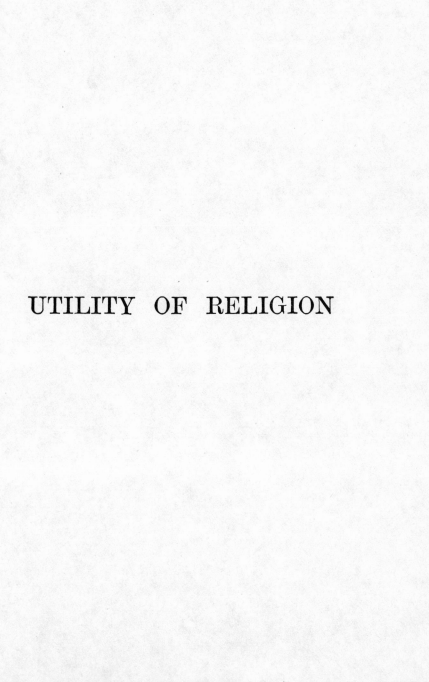

# UTILITY OF RELIGION

# UTILITY

OF

# RELIGION

IT has sometimes been remarked how much has been
written, both by friends and enemies, concerning
the truth of religion, and how little, at least in the
way of discussion or controversy, concerning its usefulness. This, however, might have been expected;
for the truth, in matters which so deeply affect us, is
our first concernment. If religion, or any particular
form of it, is true, its usefulness follows without other
proof. If to know authentically in what order of
things, under what government of the universe it is
our destiny to live, were not useful, it is difficult to
imagine what could be considered so. Whether a
person is in a pleasant or in an unpleasant place, a
palace or a prison, it cannot be otherwise than useful
to him to know where he is. So long, therefore, as
men accepted the teachings of their religion as positive facts, no more a matter of doubt than their own
existence or the existence of the objects around them,

to ask the use of believing it could not possibly occur to them. The utility of religion did not need to be asserted until the arguments for its truth had in a great measure ceased to convince. People must either have ceased to believe, or have ceased to rely on the belief of others, before they could take that inferior ground of defence without a consciousness of lowering what they were endeavouring to raise. An argument for the utility of religion is an appeal to unbelievers, to induce them to practise a well meant hypocrisy, or to semi-believers to make them avert their eyes from what might possibly shake their unstable belief, or finally to persons in general to abstain from expressing any doubts they may feel, since a fabric of immense importance to mankind is so insecure at its foundations, that men must hold their breath in its neighbourhood for fear of blowing it down.

In the present period of history, however, we seem to have arrived at a time when, among the arguments for and against religion, those which relate to its usefulness assume an important place. We are in an age of weak beliefs, and in which such belief as men have is much more determined by their wish to believe than by any mental appreciation of evidence. The wish to believe does not arise only from selfish but often from the most disinterested feelings; and though it cannot produce the unwavering and perfect reliance which once existed, it fences round all that remains of the impressions of early education ; it often causes direct misgivings to fade away by disuse ; and above all, it induces people to continue laying out their lives according to doctrines which have lost part of their hold on the mind, and to maintain towards the world the same, or a rather more demonstrative attitude of belief, than they thought it necessary to exhibit when their personal conviction was more complete.

If religious belief be indeed so necessary to mankind, as we are continually assured that it is, there is great reason to lament, that the intellectual grounds of it should require to be backed by moral bribery or subornation of the understanding. Such a state of things is most uncomfortable even for those who may, without actual insincerity, describe themselves as believers ; and still worse as regards those who, having consciously ceased to find the evidences of religion convincing, are withheld from saying so lest they should aid in doing an irreparable injury to mankind. It is a most painful position to a conscientious and cultivated mind, to be drawn in contrary directions by the two noblest of all objects of pursuit, truth, and the general good. Such a conflict must inevitably produce a growing indifference to one or other of these objects, most probably to both. Many who could render giant's service both to truth and to mankind if they believed that they could serve the

one without loss to the other, are either totally para-
lysed, or led to confine their exertions to matters of
minor detail, by the apprehension that any real freedom of speculation, or any considerable strengthening
or enlargement of the thinking faculties of mankind
at large, might, by making them unbelievers, be the
surest way to render them vicious and miserable.
Many, again, having observed in others or experienced
in themselves elevated feelings which they imagine
incapable of emanating from any other source than
religion, have an honest aversion to anything tending,
as they think, to dry up the fountain of such feelings.
They, therefore, either dislike and disparage all philosophy, or addict themselves with intolerant zeal to
those forms of it in which intuition usurps the place
of evidence, and internal feeling is made the test of
objective truth.  The whole of the prevalent metaphysics of the present century is one tissue of
suborned evidence in favour of religion; often of
Deism only, but in any case involving a misapplica-
tion of noble impulses and speculative capacities,
among the most deplorable of those wretched wastes
of human faculties which make us wonder that enough
is left to keep mankind progressive, at however slow
a pace.  It is time to consider, more impartially and
therefore more deliberately than is usually done,
whether all this straining to prop up beliefs which
require so great an expense of intellectual toil and

ingenuity to keep them standing, yields any sufficient
return in human well being; and whether that end
would not be better served by a frank recognition
that certain subjects are inaccessible to our faculties,
and by the application of the same mental powers to
the strengthening and enlargement of those òther
sources of virtue and happiness which stand in no
need of the support or sanction of supernatural beliefs
and inducements.

Neither, on the other hand, can the difficulties of
the question be so promptly disposed of, as sceptical
philosophers are sometimes inclined to believe. It is
not enough to aver, in general terms, that there
never can be any conflict between truth and utility;
that if religion be false, nothing but good can be the
consequence of rejecting it. For, though the knowledge of every positive truth is an useful acquisition,
this doctrine cannot without reservation be applied to
negative truth. When the only truth ascertainable
is that nothing can be known, we do not, by this
knowledge, gain any new fact by which to guide
ourselves; we are, at best, only disabused of our
trust in some former guide-mark, which, though
itself fallacious, may have pointed in the same
direction with the best indications we have, and if it
happens to be more conspicuous and legible, may
have kept us right when they might have been overlooked. It is, in short, perfectly conceivable that

religion may be morally useful without being intellectually sustainable: and it would be a proof of great prejudice in any unbeliever to deny, that there have been ages, and that there are still both nations and individuals, with regard to whom this is actually the case. Whether it is the case generally, and with reference to the future, it is the object of this paper to examine. We propose to inquire whether the belief in religion, considered as a mere persuasion, apart from the question of its truth, is really indispensable to the temporal welfare of mankind; whether the usefulness of the belief is intrinsic and universal, or local, temporary, and, in some sense, accidental; and whether the benefits which it yields might not be obtained otherwise, without the very large alloy of evil, by which, even in the best form of the belief, those benefits are qualified.

With the arguments on one side of the question we all are familiar : religious writers have not neglected to celebrate to the utmost the advantages both of religion in general and of their own religious faith in particular. But those who have held the contrary opinion have generally contented themselves with insisting on the more obvious and flagrant of the positive evils which have been engendered by past and present forms of religious belief. And, in truth, mankind have been so unremittingly occupied in doing evil to one another in the name of religion, from the sacrifice of Iphigenia to the Dragonnades of Louis XIV. (not to descend lower), that for any immediate purpose there was little need to seek arguments further off. These odious consequences, however, do not belong to religion in itself, but to particular forms of it, and afford no argument against the usefulness of any religions except those by which such enormities are encouraged. Moreover, the worst of these evils are already in a great measure extirpated from the more improved forms of religion; and as mankind advance in ideas and in feelings, this process of extirpation continually goes on : the immoral, or otherwise mischievous consequences which have been drawn from religion, are, one by one, abandoned, and, after having been long fought for as of its very essence, are discovered to be easily separable from it. These mischiefs, indeed, after they are past, though no longer arguments against religion, remain valid as large abatements from its beneficial influence, by showing that some of the greatest improvements ever made in the moral sentiments of mankind have taken place without it and in spite of it, and that what we are taught to regard as the chief of all improving influences, has in practice fallen so far short of such a character, that one of the hardest burdens laid upon the other good influences of human nature has been that of improving religion itself. The improvement, however, has taken place; it is still proceeding, and for the sake of fairness it should be assumed to be complete. We ought to suppose religion to have accepted the best human morality which reason and goodness can work out, from philosophical, christian, or any other elements. When it has thus freed itself from the pernicious consequences which result from its identification with any bad moral doctrine, the ground is clear for considering whether its useful properties are exclusively inherent in it, or their benefits can be obtained without it.

This essential portion of the inquiry into the temporal usefulness of religion, is the subject of the present Essay. It is a part which has been little treated of by sceptical writers. The only direct discussion of it with which I am acquainted, is in a short treatise, understood to have been partly compiled from manuscripts of Mr. Bentham,* and abounding in just and profound views; but which, as it appears to me, presses many parts of the argument too hard. This treatise, and the incidental remarks scattered through the writings of M. Comte, are the only sources known to me from which anything very pertinent to the subject can be made available for the sceptical side of the argument. I shall use both of them freely in the sequel of the present discourse.

---

* "Analysis of the Influence of Natural Religion on the Temporal Happiness of Mankind." By Philip Beauchamp.

The inquiry divides itself into two parts, corresponding to the double aspect of the subject; its social, and its individual aspect. What does religion do for society, and what for the individual? What amount of benefit to social interests, in the ordinary sense of the phrase, arises from religious belief? And what influence has it in improving and ennobling individual human nature?

The first question is interesting to everybody; the latter only to the best; but to them it is, if there be any difference, the more important of the two. We shall begin with the former, as being that which best admits of being easily brought to a precise issue.

To speak first, then, of religious belief as an instrument of social good. We must commence by drawing a distinction most commonly overlooked. It is usual to credit religion *as such* with the whole of the power inherent in *any* system of moral duties inculcated by education and enforced by opinion. Undoubtedly mankind would be in a deplorable state if no principles or precepts of justice, veracity, beneficence, were taught publicly or privately, and if these virtues were not encouraged, and the opposite vices repressed, by the praise and blame, the favourable and unfavourable sentiments, of mankind. And since nearly everything of this sort which does take place, takes place in the name of religion; since almost all who are taught any morality whatever, have it taught to them *as* religion, and inculcated on them through life principally in that character; the effect which the teaching produces as teaching, it is supposed to produce as religious teaching, and religion receives the credit of all the influence in human affairs which belongs to any generally accepted system of rules for the guidance and government of human life.

Few persons have sufficiently considered how great an influence this is; what vast efficacy belongs naturally to any doctrine received with tolerable unanimity as true, and impressed on the mind from the earliest childhood as duty. A little reflection will, I think, lead us to the conclusion that it is this which is the great moral power in human affairs, and that religion only seems so powerful because this mighty power has been under its command.

Consider first, the enormous influence of authority on the human mind. I am now speaking of involuntary influence; effect on men's conviction, on their persuasion, on their involuntary sentiments. Authority is the evidence on which the mass of mankind believe everything which they are said to know, except facts of which their own senses have taken cognizance. It is the evidence on which even the wisest receive all those truths of science, or facts in history or in life, of which they have not personally examined the proofs. Over the immense majority of human beings, the general concurrence of mankind, in any matter of opinion, is all powerful. Whatever is thus certified to them, they believe with a fulness of assurance which they do not accord even to the evidence of their senses when the general opinion of mankind stands in opposition to it. When, therefore, any rule of life and duty, whether grounded or not on religion, has conspicuously received the general assent, it obtains a hold on the belief of every individual, stronger than it would have even if he had arrived at it by the inherent force of his own understanding. If Novalis could say, not without a real meaning, "My belief has gained infinitely to me from the moment when one other human being has begun to believe the same," how much more when it is not one other person, but all the human beings whom one knows of. Some may urge it as an objection, that no scheme of morality has this universal assent, and that none, therefore, can be indebted to this source for whatever power it possesses over the mind. So far as relates to the present age, the assertion is true, and strengthens the argument which it might at first seem to controvert; for exactly in proportion as the received systems of belief have been contested, and it has become known that they have many dissentients, their hold on the general belief has been loosened, and their practical influence on conduct has declined : and since this has happened to them notwithstanding the religious sanction which attached to them, there can be no stronger evidence that they were powerful not as

religion, but as beliefs generally accepted by mankind.
To find people who believe their religion as a person
believes that fire will burn his hand when thrust into
it, we must seek them in those Oriental countries
where Europeans do not yet predominate, or in the
European world when it was still universally Catholic.
Men often disobeyed their religion in those times,
because their human passions and appetites were too
strong for it, or because the religion itself afforded
means of indulgence to breaches of its obligations;
but though they disobeyed, they, for the most part,
did not doubt.   There was in those days an absolute
and unquestioning completeness of belief, never since
general in Europe.

Such being the empire exercised over mankind by
simple authority, the mere belief and testimony of
their fellow creatures; consider next how tremendous
is the power of education; how unspeakable is the
effect of bringing people up from infancy in a belief,
and in habits founded on it.   Consider also that in
all countries, and from the earliest ages down to the
present, not merely those who are called, in a restricted sense of the term, the educated, but all or
nearly all who have been brought up by parents, or
by any one interested in them, have been taught
from their earliest years some kind of religious belief,
and some precepts as the commands of the heavenly
powers to them and to mankind.   And as it cannot

be imagined that the commands of God are to young children anything more than the commands of their parents, it is reasonable to think that any system of social duty which mankind might adopt, even though divorced from religion, would have the same advantage of being inculcated from childhood, and would have it hereafter much more perfectly than any doctrine has it at present, society being far more disposed than formerly to take pains for the moral tuition of those numerous classes whose education it has hitherto left very much to chance. Now it is especially characteristic of the impressions of early education, that they possess what it is so much more difficult for later convictions to obtain—command over the feelings. We see daily how powerful a hold these first impressions retain over the feelings even of those, who have given up the opinions which they were early taught. While on the other hand, it is only persons of a much higher degree of natural sensibility and intellect combined than it is at all common to meet with, whose feelings entwine themselves with anything like the same force round opinions which they have adopted from their own investigations later in life ; and even when they do, we may say with truth that it is because the strong sense of moral duty, the sincerity, courage and self-devotion which enabled them to do so, were themselves the fruits of early impressions.

The power of education is almost boundless : there is not one natural inclination which it is not strong enough to coerce, and, if needful, to destroy by disuse. In the greatest recorded victory which education has ever achieved over a whole host of natural inclinations in an entire people—the maintenance through centuries of the institutions of Lycurgus,—it was very little, if even at all, indebted to religion : for the Gods of the Spartans were the same as those of other Greek states ; and though, no doubt, every state of Greece believed that its particular polity had at its first establishment, some sort of divine sanction (mostly that of the Delphian oracle), there was seldom any difficulty in obtaining the same or an equally powerful sanction for a change. It was not religion which formed the strength of the Spartan institutions : the root of the system was devotion to Sparta, to the ideal of the country or State : which transformed into ideal devotion to a greater country, the world, would be equal to that and far nobler achievements. Among the Greeks generally, social morality was extremely independent of religion. The inverse relation was rather that which existed between them ; the worship of the Gods was inculcated chiefly as a social duty, inasmuch as if they were neglected or insulted, it was believed that their displeasure would fall not more upon the offending individual than upon the state or community which bred and tolerated him. Such moral teaching as existed in Greece had very little to do with religion. The Gods were not supposed to concern themselves much with men's conduct to one another, except when men had contrived to make the Gods themselves an interested party, by placing an assertion or an engagement under the sanction of a solemn appeal to them, by oath or vow. I grant that the sophists and philosophers, and even popular orators, did their best to press religion into the service of their special objects, and to make it be thought that the sentiments of whatever kind, which they were engaged in inculcating, were particularly acceptable to the Gods, but this never seems the primary consideration in any case save those of direct offence to the dignity of the Gods themselves. For the enforcement of human moralities secular inducements were almost exclusively relied on. The case of Greece is, I believe, the only one in which any teaching, other than religious, has had the unspeakable advantage of forming the basis of education : and though much may be said against the quality of some part of the teaching, very little can be said against its effectiveness. The most memorable example of the power of education over conduct, is afforded (as I have just remarked) by this exceptional case ; constituting a strong presumption that in other cases, early religious teaching has owed its power over mankind rather to its being early than to its being religious.

We have now considered two powers, that of authority, and that of early education, which operate through men's involuntary beliefs, feelings and desires, and which religion has hitherto held as its almost exclusive appanage. Let us now consider a third power which operates directly on their actions, whether their involuntary sentiments are carried with it or not. This is the power of public opinion; of the praise and blame, the favour and disfavour, of their fellow creatures; and is a source of strength inherent in any system of moral belief which is generally adopted, whether connected with religion or not.

Men are so much accustomed to give to the motives that decide their actions, more flattering names than justly belong to them, that they are generally quite unconscious how much those parts of their conduct which they most pride themselves on (as well as some which they are ashamed of), are determined by the motive of public opinion. Of course public opinion for the most part enjoins the same things which are enjoined by the received social morality ; that morality being, in truth, the summary of the conduct which each one of the multitude, whether he himself observes it with any strictness or not, desires that others should observe towards him. People are therefore easily able to flatter themselves that they are acting from the motive of conscience when they are doing in obedience to the inferior motive, things which their conscience approves. We continually see how great is the power of opinion in opposition to conscience; how men "follow a multitude to do evil;" how often opinion induces them to do what their conscience disapproves, and still oftener prevents them from doing what it commands. But when the motive of public opinion acts in the same direction with conscience, which, since it has usually itself made the conscience in the first instance, it for the most part naturally does; it is then, of all motives which operate on the bulk of mankind, the most overpowering.

The names of all the strongest passions (except the merely animal ones) manifested by human nature, are each of them a name for some one part only of the motive derived from what I here call public opinion. The love of glory; the love of praise; the love of admiration; the love of respect and deference; even the love of sympathy, are portions of its attractive power. Vanity is a vituperative name for its attractive influence generally, when considered excessive in degree. The fear of shame, the dread of ill repute or of being disliked or hated, are the direct and simple forms of its deterring power. But the deterring force of the unfavourable sentiments of mankind does not consist solely in the painfulness of knowing oneself to be the object of those sentiments; it includes all the penalties which they can inflict: exclusion from social

intercourse and from the innumerable good offices
which human beings require from one another; the
forfeiture of all that is called success in life; often
the great diminution or total loss of means of subsistence; positive ill offices of various kinds, sufficient
to render life miserable, and reaching in some states
of society as far as actual persecution to death. And
again the attractive, or impelling influence of public
opinion, includes the whole range of what is commonly meant by ambition: for, except in times of
lawless military violence, the objects of social
ambition can only be attained by means of the good
opinion and favourable disposition of our fellow-
creatures; nor, in nine cases out of ten, would those
objects be even desired, were it not for the power
they confer over the sentiments of mankind. Even
the pleasure of self-approbation, in the great majority,
is mainly dependent on the opinion of others. Such
is the involuntary influence of authority on ordinary
minds, that persons must be of a better than ordinary
mould to be capable of a full assurance that they are
in the right, when the world, that is, when *their*
world, thinks them wrong: nor is there, to most
men, any proof so demonstrative of their own virtue
or talent as that people in general seem to believe in
it. Through all departments of human affairs, regard
for the sentiments of our fellow-creatures is in one
shape or other, in nearly all characters, the pervading

motive. And we ought to note that this motive is naturally strongest in the most sensitive natures, which are the most promising material for the formation of great virtues. How far its power reaches is known by too familiar experience to require either proof or illustration here. When once the means of living have been obtained, the far greater part of the remaining labour and effort which takes place on the earth, has for its object to acquire the respect or the favourable regard of mankind; to be looked up to, or at all events, not to be looked down upon by them. The industrial and commercial activity which advance civilization, the frivolity, prodigality, and selfish thirst of aggrandizement which retard it, flow equally from that source. While as an instance of the power exercised by the terrors derived from public opinion, we know how many murders have been committed merely to remove a witness who knew and was likely to disclose some secret that would bring disgrace upon his murderer.

Any one who fairly and impartially considers the subject, will see reason to believe that those great effects on human conduct, which are commonly ascribed to motives derived directly from religion, have mostly for their proximate cause the influence of human opinion. Religion has been powerful not by its intrinsic force, but because it has wielded that additional and more mighty power. The effect of religion has been immense in giving a direction to public opinion: which has, in many most important respects, been wholly determined by it. But without the sanctions superadded by public opinion, its own proper sanctions have never, save in exceptional characters, or in peculiar moods of mind, exercised a very potent influence, after the times had gone by, in which divine agency was supposed habitually to employ temporal rewards and punishments. When a man firmly believed that if he violated the sacredness of a particular sanctuary he would be struck dead on the spot, or smitten suddenly with a mortal disease, he doubtless took care not to incur the penalty: but when any one had had the courage to defy the danger, and escaped with impunity, the spell was broken. If ever any people were taught that they were under a divine government, and that unfaithfulness to their religion and law would be visited from above with temporal chastisements, the Jews were so. Yet their history was a mere succession of lapses into Paganism. Their prophets and historians, who held fast to the ancient beliefs (though they gave them so liberal an interpretation as to think it a sufficient manifestation of God's displeasure towards a king if any evil happened to his great grandson), never ceased to complain that their countrymen turned a deaf ear to their vaticinations; and hence, with the faith they held in a divine govern-

ment operating by temporal penalties, they could not
fail to anticipate (as Mirabeau's father without such
prompting, was able to do on the eve of the French
Revolution) *la culbute générale;* an expectation which,
luckily for the credit of their prophetic powers, was
fulfilled; unlike that of the Apostle John, who in the
only intelligible prophecy in the Revelations, foretold
to the city of the seven hills a fate like that of
Nineveh and Babylon; which prediction remains to
this hour unaccomplished. Unquestionably the conviction which experience in time forced on all but
the very ignorant, that divine punishments were
not to be confidently expected in a temporal form,
contributed much to the downfall of the old religions,
and the general adoption of one which without absolutely excluding providential interferences in this life
for the punishment of guilt or the reward of merit,
removed the principal scene of divine retribution to
a world after death. But rewards and punishments
postponed to that distance of time, and never seen by
the eye, are not calculated, even when infinite and
eternal, to have, on ordinary minds, a very powerful
effect in opposition to strong temptation. Their
remoteness alone is a prodigious deduction from their
efficacy, on such minds as those which most require
the restraint of punishment. A still greater abatement is their uncertainty, which belongs to them
from the very nature of the case: for rewards and

punishments administered after death, must be awarded
not definitely to particular actions, but on a general
survey of the person's whole life, and he easily per-
suades himself that whatever may have been his
peccadilloes, there will be a balance in his favour at
the last. All positive religions aid this self-delusion.
Bad religions teach that divine vengeance may be
bought off, by offerings, or personal abasement; the
better religions, not to drive sinners to despair, dwell
so much on the divine mercy, that hardly any one
is compelled to think himself irrevocably condemned.
The sole quality in these punishments which might
seem calculated to make them efficacious, their overpowering magnitude, is itself a reason why nobody
(except a hypochondriac here and there) ever really
believes that he is in any very serious danger of
incurring them. Even the worst malefactor is hardly
able to think that any crime he has had it in his power
to commit, any evil he can have inflicted in this short
space of existence, can have deserved torture extending
through an eternity. Accordingly religious writers
and preachers are never tired of complaining how
little effect religious motives have on men's lives and
conduct, notwithstanding the tremendous penalties
denounced.

Mr. Bentham, whom I have already mentioned as
one of the few authors who have written anything to
the purpose on the efficacy of the religious sanction,

adduces several cases to prove that religious obligation, when not enforced by public opinion, produces scarcely any effect on conduct. His first example is that of oaths. The oaths taken in courts of justice, and any others which from the manifest importance to society of their being kept, public opinion rigidly enforces, are felt as real and binding obligations. But university oaths and custom-house oaths, though in a religious point of view equally obligatory, are in practice utterly disregarded even by men in other respects honourable. The university oath to obey the statutes has been for centuries, with universal acquiescence, set at nought: and utterly false statements are (or used to be) daily and unblushingly sworn to at the Custom-house, by persons as attentive as other people to all the ordinary obligations of life. The explanation being, that veracity in these cases was not enforced by public opinion. The second case which Bentham cites is duelling; a practice now, in this country, obsolete, but in full vigour in several other christian countries; deemed and admitted to be a sin by almost all who, nevertheless, in obedience to opinion, and to escape from personal humiliation, are guilty of it. The third case is that of illicit sexual intercourse; which in both sexes, stands in the very highest rank of religious sins, yet not being severely censured by opinion in the male sex, they have in general very little scruple in committing it; while in the case of women, though the religious obligation is not stronger, yet being backed in real earnest by public opinion, it is commonly effectual.

Some objection may doubtless be taken to Bentham's instances, considered as crucial experiments on the power of the religious sanction; for (it may be said) people do not really believe that in these cases they shall be punished by God, any more than by man. And this is certainly true in the case of those university and other oaths, which are habitually taken without any intention of keeping them. The oath, in these cases, is regarded as a mere formality, destitute of any serious meaning in the sight of the Deity; and the most scrupulous person, even if he does reproach himself for having taken an oath which nobody deems fit to be kept, does not in his conscience tax himself with the guilt of perjury, but only with the profanation of a ceremony. This, therefore, is not a good example of the weakness of the religious motive when divorced from that of human opinion. The point which it illustrates is rather the tendency of the one motive to come and go with the other, so that where the penalties of public opinion cease, the religious motive ceases also. The same criticism, however, is not equally applicable to Bentham's other examples, duelling, and sexual irregularities. Those who do these acts, the first by the command of public opinion, the latter with its indulgence, really do, in most cases, believe that they are offending God. Doubtless, they do not think that they are offending him in such a degree as very seriously to endanger their salvation. Their reliance on his mercy prevails over their dread of his resentment; affording an exemplification of the remark already made, that the unavoidable uncertainty of religious penalties makes them feeble as a deterring motive. They are so, even in the case of acts which human opinion condemns : much more, with those to which it is indulgent. What mankind think venial, it is hardly ever supposed that God looks upon in a serious light : at least by those who feel in themselves any inclination to practise it.

I do not for a moment think of denying that there are states of mind in which the idea of religious punishment acts with the most overwhelming force. In hypochondriacal disease, and in those with whom, from great disappointments or other moral causes, the thoughts and imagination have assumed an habitually melancholy complexion, that topic, falling in with the pre-existing tendency of the mind, supplies images well fitted to drive the unfortunate sufferer even to madness. Often, during a temporary state of depression, these ideas take such a hold of the mind as to give a permanent turn to the character; being the most common case of what, in sectarian phraseology, is called conversion. But if the depressed state ceases after the conversion, as it commonly does, and the convert does not relapse, but perseveres in his new course of life, the principal difference between it and the old is usually found to be, that the man now guides his life by the public opinion of his religious associates, as he before guided it by that of the profane world. At all events, there is one clear proof how little the generality of mankind, either religious or worldly, really dread eternal punishments, when we see how, even at the approach of death, when the remoteness which took so much from their effect has been exchanged for the closest proximity, almost all persons who have not been guilty of some enormous crime (and many who have) are quite free from uneasiness as to their prospects in another world, and never for a moment seem to think themselves in any real danger of eternal punishment.

With regard to the cruel deaths and bodily tortures, which confessors and martyrs have so often undergone for the sake of religion, I would not depreciate them by attributing any part of this admirable courage and constancy to the influence of human opinion. Human opinion indeed has shown itself quite equal to the production of similar firmness in persons not otherwise distinguished by moral excellence; such as the North American Indian at the stake. But if it was not the thought of glory in the eyes of their fellow-religionists, which upheld these

heroic sufferers in their agony, as little do I believe
that it was, generally speaking, that of the pleasures
of heaven or the pains of hell.  Their impulse was a
divine enthusiasm—a self-forgetting devotion to an
idea : a state of exalted feeling, by no means peculiar
to religion, but which it is the privilege of every
great cause to inspire; a phenomenon belonging to
the critical moments of existence, not to the ordinary
play of human motives, and from which nothing can
be inferred as to the efficacy of the ideas which it
sprung from, whether religious or any other, in overcoming ordinary temptations, and regulating the course
of daily life.

We may now have done with this branch of the
subject, which is, after all, the vulgarest part of it.
The value of religion as a supplement to human laws,
a more cunning sort of police, an auxiliary to the
thief-catcher and the hangman, is not that part of its
claims which the more highminded of its votaries are
fondest of insisting on : and they would probably be
as ready as any one to admit, that if the nobler offices
of religion in the soul could be dispensed with, a
substitute might be found for so coarse and selfish a
social instrument as the fear of hell.  In their view
of the matter, the best of mankind absolutely require
religion for the perfection of their own character, even
though the coercion of the worst might possibly be
accomplished without its aid.

Even in the social point of view, however, under its most elevated aspect, these nobler spirits generally assert the necessity of religion, as a teacher, if not as an enforcer, of social morality. They say, that religion alone can teach us what morality is; that all the high morality ever recognized by mankind, was learnt from religion; that the greatest uninspired philosophers in their sublimest flights, stopt far short of the christian morality, and whatever inferior morality they may have attained to (by the assistance, as many think, of dim traditions derived from the Hebrew books, or from a primæval revelation) they never could induce the common mass of their fellow citizens to accept it from them. That, only when a morality is understood to come from the Gods, do men in general adopt it, rally round it, and lend their human sanctions for its enforcement. That granting the sufficiency of human motives to make the rule obeyed, were it not for the religious idea we should not have had the rule itself.

There is truth in much of this, considered as matter of history. Ancient peoples have generally, if not always, received their morals, their laws, their intellectual beliefs, and even their practical arts of life, all in short which tended either to guide or to discipline them, as revelations from the superior powers, and in any other way could not easily have been induced to accept them. This was partly the effect of their hopes and fears from those powers, which were of much greater and more universal potency in early times, when the agency of the Gods was seen in the daily events of life, experience not having yet disclosed the fixed laws according to which physical phenomena succeed one another. Independently, too, of personal hopes and fears, the involuntary deference felt by these rude minds for power superior to their own, and the tendency to suppose that beings of superhuman power must also be of superhuman knowledge and wisdom, made them disinterestedly desire to conform their conduct to the presumed preferences of these powerful beings, and to adopt no new practice without their authorization either spontaneously given, or solicited and obtained.

But because, when men were still savages, they would not have received either moral or scientific truths unless they had supposed them to be supernaturally imparted, does it follow that they would now give up moral truths any more than scientific, because they believed them to have no higher origin than wise and noble human hearts? Are not moral truths strong enough in their own evidence, at all events to retain the belief of mankind when once they have acquired it? I grant that some of the precepts of Christ as exhibited in the Gospels—rising far above the Paulism which is the foundation of ordinary Christianity—carry some kinds of moral goodness to a greater height than had ever been attained before, though much even of what is supposed to be peculiar to them is equalled in the Meditations of Marcus Antoninus, which we have no ground for believing to have been in any way indebted to Christianity. But this benefit, whatever it amounts to, has been gained. Mankind have entered into the possession of it. It has become the property of humanity, and cannot now be lost by anything short of a return to primæval barbarism. The "new commandment to love one another;"* the recognition that the 'greatest are those who serve, not who are served by, others ; the reverence for the weak and humble, which is the foundation of chivalry, they and not the strong being pointed out as having the first place in God's regard, and the first claim on their fellow men; the lesson of the parable of the Good Samaritan ; that of "he that is without sin let him throw the first stone;" the precept of doing as we would be done by ; and such other noble moralities as are to be found, mixed with some poetical exaggerations, and some maxims of which it is difficult to ascertain the precise object; in the authentic sayings of Jesus of Nazareth ; these are surely in sufficient

---

* Not, however, a new commandment. In justice to the great Hebrew lawgiver, it should always be remembered that the precept, to love thy neighbour as thyself, already existed in the Pentateuch; and very surprising it is to find it there.

harmony with the intellect and feelings of every good man or woman, to be in no danger of being let go, after having been once acknowledged as the creed of the best and foremost portion of our species. There will be, as there have been, shortcomings enough for a long time to come in acting on them; but that they should be forgotten, or cease to be operative on the human conscience, while human beings remain cultivated or civilized, may be pronounced, once for all, impossible.

On the other hand, there is a very real evil consequent on ascribing a supernatural origin to the received maxims of morality. That origin consecrates the whole of them, and protects them from being discussed or criticized. So that if among the moral doctrines received as a part of religion, there be any which are imperfect — which were either erroneous from the first, or not properly limited and guarded in the expression, or which, unexceptionable once, are no longer suited to the changes that have taken place in human relations (and it is my firm belief that in so-called christian morality, instances of all these kinds are to be found) these doctrines are considered equally binding on the conscience with the noblest, most permanent and most universal precepts of Christ. Wherever morality is supposed to be of supernatural origin, morality is stereotyped; as law is, for the same reason, among believers in the Koran.

Belief, then, in the supernatural, great as are the services which it rendered in the early stages of human development, cannot be considered to be any longer required, either for enabling us to know what is right and wrong in social morality, or for supplying us with motives to do right and to abstain from wrong. Such belief, therefore, is not necessary for social purposes, at least in the coarse way in which these can be considered apart from the character of the individual human being. That more elevated branch of the subject now remains to be considered. If supernatural beliefs are indeed necessary to the perfection of the individual character, they are necessary also to the highest excellence in social conduct: necessary in a far higher sense than that vulgar one, which constitutes it the great support of morality in common eyes.

Let us then consider, what it is in human nature which causes it to require a religion; what wants of the human mind religion supplies, and what qualities it developes. When we have understood this, we shall be better able to judge, how far these wants can be otherwise supplied and those qualities, or qualities equivalent to them, unfolded and brought to perfection by other means.

The old saying, *Primus in orbe Deos fecit timor*, I hold to be untrue, or to contain, at most, only a small amount of truth. Belief in Gods had, I conceive, even in the rudest minds, a more honourable origin. Its universality has been very rationally explained from the spontaneous tendency of the mind to attribute life and volition, similar to what it feels in itself, to all natural objects and phenomena which appear to be self-moving. This was a plausible fancy, and no better theory could be formed at first. It was naturally persisted in so long as the motions and operations of these objects seemed to be arbitrary, and incapable of being accounted for but by the free choice of the Power itself. At first, no doubt, the objects themselves were supposed to be alive; and this belief still subsists among African fetish-worshippers. But as it must soon have appeared absurd that things which could do so much more than man, could not or would not do what man does, as for example to speak, the transition was made to supposing that the object present to the senses was inanimate, but was the creature and instrument of an invisible being with a form and organs similar to the human.

These beings having first been believed in, fear of them necessarily followed; since they were thought able to inflict at pleasure on human beings great evils, which the sufferers neither knew how to avert nor to foresee, but were left dependent, for their chances of doing either, upon solicitations addressed to the deities themselves. It is true, therefore, that fear had much to do with religion: but belief in the Gods evidently

preceded, and did not arise from, fear: though the
fear, when established, was a strong support to the
belief, nothing being conceived to be so great an
offence to the divinities as any doubt of their
existence.

It is unnecessary to prosecute further the natural
history of religion, as we have not here to account for
its origin in rude minds, but for its persistency in the
cultivated. A sufficient explanation of this will, I
conceive, be found in the small limits of man's certain
knowledge, and the boundlessness of his desire to
know. Human existence is girt round with mystery :
the narrow region of our experience is a small island
in the midst of a boundless sea, which at once awes
our feelings and stimulates our imagination by its
vastness and its obscurity. To add to the mystery,
the domain of our earthly existence is not only an
island in infinite space, but also in infinite time.
The past and the future are alike shrouded from us :
we neither know the origin of anything which is, nor
its final destination. If we feel deeply interested in
knowing that there are myriads of worlds at an im-
measurable, and to our faculties inconceivable, distance
from us in space ; if we are eager to discover what
little we can about these worlds, and when we cannot
know what they are, can never satiate ourselves with
speculating on what they may be ; is it not a matter
of far deeper interest to us to learn, or even to con-

jecture, from whence came this nearer world which
we inhabit; what cause or agency made it what it is,
and on what powers depend its future fate? Who
would not desire this more ardently than any other
conceivable knowledge, so long as there appeared the
slightest hope of attaining it? What would not one
give for any credible tidings from that mysterious
region, any glimpse into it which might enable us to
see the smallest light through its darkness, especially
any theory of it which we could believe, and which
represented it as tenanted by a benignant and not a
hostile influence? But since we are able to penetrate
into that region with the imagination only, assisted
by specious but inconclusive analogies derived from
human agency and design, imagination is free to fill
up the vacancy with the imagery most congenial to
itself; sublime and elevating if it be a lofty imagination, low and mean if it be a grovelling one.

Religion and poetry address themselves, at least in
one of their aspects, to the same part of the human
constitution: they both supply the same want, that of
ideal conceptions grander and more beautiful than we
see realized in the prose of human life. Religion, as
distinguished from poetry, is the product of the
craving to know whether these imaginative conceptions have realities answering to them in some other
world than ours. The mind, in this state, eagerly
catches at any rumours respecting other worlds,

especially when delivered by persons whom it deems wiser than itself. To the poetry of the supernatural, comes to be thus added a positive belief and expectation, which unpoetical minds can share with the poetical. Belief in a God or Gods, and in a life after death, becomes the canvas which every mind, according to its capacity, covers with such ideal pictures as it can either invent or copy. In that other life each hopes to find the good which he has failed to find on earth, or the better which is suggested to him by the good which on earth he has partially seen and known. More especially, this belief supplies the finer minds with material for conceptions of beings more awful than they *can* have known on earth, and more excellent than they probably *have* known. So long as human life is insufficient to satisfy human aspirations, so long there will be a craving for higher things, which finds its most obvious satisfaction in religion. So long as earthly life is full of sufferings, so long there will be need of consolations, which the hope of heaven affords to the selfish, the love of God to the tender and grateful.

The value, therefore, of religion to the individual, both in the past and present, as a source of personal satisfaction and of elevated feelings, is not to be disputed. But it has still to be considered, whether in order to obtain this good, it is necessary to travel beyond the boundaries of the world which we inhabit;

or whether the idealization of our earthly life, the cultivation of a high conception of what *it* may be made, is not capable of supplying a poetry, and, in the best sense of the word, a religion, equally fitted to exalt the feelings, and (with the same aid from education) still better calculated to ennoble the conduct, than any belief respecting the unseen powers.

At the bare suggestion of such a possibility, many will exclaim, that the short duration, the smallness and insignificance of life, if there is no prolongation of it beyond what we see, makes it impossible that great and elevated feelings can connect themselves with anything laid out on so small a scale: that such a conception of life can match with nothing higher than Epicurean feelings, and the Epicurean doctrine " Let us eat and drink, for to-morrow we die."

Unquestionably, within certain limits, the maxim of the Epicureans is sound, and applicable to much higher things than eating and drinking. To make the most of the present for all good purposes, those of enjoyment among the rest; to keep under control those mental dispositions which lead to undue sacrifice of present good for a future which may never arrive; to cultivate the habit of deriving pleasure from things within our reach, rather than from the too eager pursuit of objects at a distance; to think all time wasted which is not spent either in personal pleasure or in doing things useful to oneself or others; these are wise maxims, and the " carpe diem" doctrine, carried thus far, is a rational and legitimate corollary from the shortness of life. But that because life is short we should care for nothing beyond it, is not a legitimate conclusion ; and the supposition, that human beings in general are not capable of feeling deep and even the deepest interest in things which they will never live to see, is a view of human nature as false as it is abject. Let it be remembered that if individual life is short, the life of the human species is not short; its indefinite duration is practically equivalent to endlessness ; and being combined with indefinite capability of improvement, it offers to the imagination and sympathies a large enough object to satisfy any reasonable demand for grandeur of aspiration. If such an object appears small to a mind accustomed to dream of infinite and eternal beatitudes,it will expand into far other dimensions when those baseless fancies shall have receded into the past.

Nor let it be thought that only the more eminent of our species, in mind and heart, are capable of identifying their feelings with the entire life of the human race. This noble capability implies indeed a certain cultivation, but not superior to that which might be, and certainly will be if human improvement continues, the lot of all. Objects far smaller than this, and equally confined within the limits of the earth (though not within those of a single human life), have been found sufficient to inspire large masses and long successions of mankind with an enthusiasm capable of ruling the conduct, and colouring the whole life. Rome was to the entire Roman people, for many generations as much a religion as Jehovah was to the Jews; nay, much more, for they never fell off from their worship as the Jews did from theirs. And the Romans, otherwise a selfish people, with no very remarkable faculties of any kind except the purely practical, derived nevertheless from this one idea a certain greatness of soul, which manifests itself in all their history where that idea is concerned and no-where else, and has earned for them the large share of admiration, in other respects not at all deserved, which has been felt for them by most noble-minded persons from that time to this.

When we consider how ardent a sentiment, in favourable circumstances of education, the love of country has become, we cannot judge it impossible that the love of that larger country, the world, may be nursed into similar strength, both as a source of elevated emotion and as a principle of duty. He who needs any other lesson on this subject than the whole course of ancient history affords, let him read Cicero *de Officiis*. It cannot be said that the standard of morals laid down in that celebrated treatise is a high standard. To our notions it is on many points unduly lax, and admits capitulations of conscience. But on the subject of duty to our country there is no compromise. That any man, with the smallest pretensions to virtue, could hesitate to sacrifice life, reputation, family, everything valuable to him, to the love of country is a supposition which this eminent interpreter of Greek and Roman morality cannot entertain for a moment. If, then, persons could be trained, as we see they were, not only to believe in theory that the good of their country was an object to which all others ought to yield, but to feel this practically as the grand duty of life, so also may they be made to feel the same absolute obligation towards the universal good. A morality grounded on large and wise views of the good of the whole, neither sacrificing the individual to the aggregate nor the aggregate to the individual, but giving to duty on the one hand and to freedom and spontaneity on the other their proper province, would derive its power in the superior natures from sympathy and benevolence and the passion for ideal excellence: in the inferior, from the same feelings cultivated up to the measure of their capacity, with the superadded force of shame. This exalted morality would not depend for its ascendancy on any hope of reward; but the reward which might be looked for, and the thought of which would be a consolation in suffering, and a support in moments of weakness, would not be a problematical future existence, but the approbation, in this, of those whom we respect, and ideally of all those, dead or living, whom we admire or venerate. For, the thought that our dead parents or friends would have approved our conduct is a scarcely less powerful motive than the knowledge that our living ones do approve it : and the idea that Socrates, or Howard or Washington, or Antoninus, or Christ, would have sympathized with us, or that we are attempting to do our part in the spirit in which they did theirs, has operated on the very best minds, as a strong incentive to act up to their highest feelings and convictions.

To call these sentiments by the name morality, exclusively of any other title, is claiming too little for them. They are a real religion ; of which, as of other religions, outward good works (the utmost meaning usually suggested by the word morality) are only a part, and are indeed rather the fruits of the religion than the religion itself. The essence of religion is the strong and earnest direction of the emotions and desires towards an ideal object, recognized as of the highest excellence, and as rightfully paramount over all selfish objects of desire. This condition is fulfilled by the Religion of Humanity in as eminent a degree, and in as high a sense, as by the supernatural religions even in their best manifestations, and far more so than in any of their others.

Much more might be added on this topic; but

enough has been said to convince any one, who can distinguish between the intrinsic capacities of human nature and the forms in which those capacities happen to have been historically developed, that the sense of unity with mankind, and a deep feeling for the general good, may be cultivated into a sentiment and a principle capable of fulfilling every important function of religion and itself justly entitled to the name. I will now further maintain, that it is not only capable of fulfilling these functions, but would fulfil them better than any form whatever of supernaturalism. It is not only entitled to be called a religion : it is a better religion than any of those which are ordinarily called by that title.

For, in the first place, it is disinterested. It carries the thoughts and feelings out of self, and fixes them on an unselfish object, loved and pursued as an end for its own sake. The religions which deal in promises and threats regarding a future life, do exactly the contrary : they fasten down the thoughts to the person's own posthumous interests ; they tempt him to regard the performance of his duties to others mainly as a means to his own personal salvation ; and are one of the most serious obstacles to the great purpose of moral culture, the strengthening of the unselfish and weakening of the selfish element in our nature ; since they hold out to the imagination selfish good and evil of such tremendous magnitude, that it is difficult for any one who fully believes in their reality, to have feeling or interest to spare for any other distant and ideal object. It is true, many of the most unselfish of mankind have been believers in supernaturalism, because their minds have not dwelt on the threats and promises of their religion, but chiefly on the idea of a Being to whom they looked up with a confiding love, and in whose hands they willingly left all that related especially to themselves. But in its effect on common minds, what now goes by the name of religion operates mainly through the feelings of self-interest. Even the Christ of the Gospels holds out the direct promise of reward from heaven as a primary inducement to the noble and beautiful beneficence towards our fellow-creatures which he so impressively inculcates. This is a radical inferiority of the best supernatural religions, compared with the Religion of Humanity; since the greatest thing which moral influences can do for the amelioration of human nature, is to cultivate the unselfish feelings in the only mode in which any active principle in human nature can be effectually cultivated, namely by habitual exercise: but the habit of expecting to be rewarded in another life for our conduct in this, makes even virtue itself no longer an exercise of the unselfish feelings.

Secondly, it is an immense abatement from the worth of the old religions as means of elevating and improving human character, that it is nearly, if not quite impossible for them to produce their best moral effects, unless we suppose a certain torpidity, if not positive twist in the intellectual faculties. For it is impossible that any one who habitually thinks, and who is unable to blunt his inquiring intellect by sophistry, should be able without misgiving to go on ascribing absolute perfection to the author and ruler of so clumsily made and capriciously governed a creation as this planet and the life of its inhabitants. The adoration of such a being cannot be with the whole heart, unless the heart is first considerably sophisticated. The worship must either be greatly overclouded by doubt, and occasionally quite darkened by it, or the moral sentiments must sink to the low level of the ordinances of Nature : the worshipper must learn to think blind partiality, atrocious cruelty, and reckless injustice, not blemishes in an object of worship, since all these abound to excess in the commonest phenomena of Nature. It is true, the God who is worshipped is not, generally speaking, the God of Nature only, but also the God of some revelation ; and the character of the revelation will greatly modify and, it may be, improve the moral influences of the religion. This is emphatically true of Christianity ; since the Author of the Sermon on the Mount is assuredly a far more benignant Being than the Author of Nature. But unfortunately, the believer in the christian revelation is obliged to believe that the same being is the author of both. This, unless he resolutely averts his mind from the subject, or practises the act of quieting his conscience by sophistry, involves him in moral perplexities without end; since the ways of his Deity in Nature are on many occasions totally at variance with the precepts, as he believes, of the same Deity in the Gospel. He who comes out with least moral damage from this embarrassment, is probably the one who never attempts to reconcile the two standards with one another, but confesses to himself that the purposes of Providence are mysterious, that its ways are not our ways, that its justice and goodness are not the justice and goodness which we can conceive and which it befits us to practise. When, however, this is the feeling of the believer, the worship of the Deity ceases to be the adoration of abstract moral perfection. It becomes the bowing down to a gigantic image of something not fit for us to imitate. It is the worship of power only.

I say nothing of the moral difficulties and perversions involved in revelation itself; though even in the Christianity of the Gospels, at least in its ordinary interpretation, there are some of so flagrant a character as almost to outweigh all the beauty and benignity and moral greatness which so eminently distinguish the sayings and character of Christ. The recognition, for example, of the object of highest worship, in a being who could make a Hell; and who could create countless generations of human beings with the certain foreknowledge that he was creating them for this fate. Is there any moral enormity which might not be justified by imitation of such a Deity? And is it possible to adore such a one without a frightful distortion of the standard of right and wrong? Any other of the outrages to the most ordinary justice and humanity involved in the common christian conception of the moral character of God, sinks into insignificance beside this dreadful idealization of wickedness. Most of them too, are happily not so unequivocally deducible from the very words of Christ as to be indisputably a part of christian doctrine. It may be doubted, for instance, whether Christianity is really responsible for atonement and redemption, original sin and vicarious punishment: and the same may be said respecting the doctrine which makes belief in the divine mission of Christ a necessary condition of salvation. It is nowhere represented that Christ himself made this statement, except in the huddled-up account of the Resurrection contained in the concluding verses of St. Mark, which some critics (I believe the best), consider to be an interpolation. Again, the proposition that "the powers that be are ordained of God" and the whole series of corollaries deduced from it in the Epistles, belong to St. Paul, and must stand or fall with Paulism, not with

Christianity. But there is one moral contradiction inseparable from every form of Christianity, which no ingenuity can resolve, and no sophistry explain away. It is, that so precious a gift, bestowed on a few, should have been withheld from the many: that countless millions of human beings should have been allowed to live and die, to sin and suffer, without the one thing needful, the divine remedy for sin and suffering, which it would have cost the Divine Giver as little to have vouchsafed to all, as to have bestowed by special grace upon a favoured minority. Add to this, that the divine message, assuming it to be such, has been authenticated by credentials so insufficient, that they fail to convince a large proportion of the strongest and most cultivated minds, and the tendency to disbelieve them appears to grow with the growth of scientific knowledge and critical discrimination. He who can believe these to be the intentional shortcomings of a perfectly good Being, must impose silence on every prompting of the sense of goodness and justice as received among men.

It is, no doubt, possible (and there are many instances of it) to worship with the intensest devotion either Deity, that of Nature or of the Gospel, without any perversion of the moral sentiments: but this must be by fixing the attention exclusively on what is beautiful and beneficent in the precepts and spirit of the Gospel and in the dispensations of Nature, and putting all that is the reverse as entirely aside as if it did not exist. Accordingly, this simple and innocent faith can only, as I have said, co-exist with a torpid and inactive state of the speculative faculties. For a person of exercised intellect, there is no way of attaining anything equivalent to it, save by sophistication and perversion, either of the understanding or of the conscience. It may almost always be said both of sects and of individuals, who derive their morality from religion, that the better logicians they are, the worse moralists.

One only form of belief in the supernatural—one only theory respecting the origin and government of the universe—stands wholly clear both of intellectual contradiction and of moral obliquity. It is that which, resigning irrevocably the idea of an omnipotent creator, regards Nature and Life not as the expression throughout of the moral character and purpose of the Deity, but as the product of a struggle between contriving goodness and an intractable material, as was believed by Plato, or a Principle of Evil, as was the doctrine of the Manicheans. A creed like this, which I have known to be devoutly held by at least one cultivated and conscientious person of our own day, allows it to be believed that all the mass of evil which exists was undesigned by, and exists not by the appointment of, but in spite of the Being whom we are called upon to worship. A virtuous human

being assumes in this theory the exalted character of
a fellow-labourer with the Highest, a fellow-combatant
in the great strife; contributing his little, which by
the aggregation of many like himself becomes much,
towards that progressive ascendancy, and ultimately
complete triumph of good over evil, which history
points to, and which this doctrine teaches us to
regard as planned by the Being to whom we owe all
the benevolent contrivance we behold in Nature.
Against the moral tendency of this creed no possible
objection can lie: it can produce on whoever can
succeed in believing it, no other than an ennobling
effect. The evidence for it, indeed, if evidence it can
be called, is too shadowy and unsubstantial, and the
promises it holds out too distant and uncertain, to
admit of its being a permanent substitute for the
religion of humanity; but the two may be held in
conjunction: and he to whom ideal good, and the
progress of the world towards it, are already a religion,
even though that other creed may seem to him a
belief not grounded on evidence, is at liberty to
indulge the pleasing and encouraging thought, that
its truth is possible. Apart from all dogmatic belief,
there is for those who need it, an ample domain in
the region of the imagination which may be planted
with possibilities, with hypotheses which cannot be
known to be false; and when there is anything in
the appearances of nature to favour them, as in this

case there is (for whatever force we attach to the analogies of Nature with the effects of human contrivance, there is no disputing the remark of Paley, that what is good in nature exhibits those analogies much oftener than what is evil), the contemplation of these possibilities is a legitimate indulgence, capable of bearing its part, with other influences, in feeding and animating the tendency of the feelings and impulses towards good.

One advantage, such as it is, the supernatural religions must always possess over the Religion of Humanity; the prospect they hold out to the individual of a life after death. For, though the scepticism of the understanding does not necessarily exclude the Theism of the imagination and feelings, and this, again, gives opportunity for a hope that the power which has done so much for us may be able and willing to do this also, such vague possibility must ever stop far short of a conviction. It remains then to estimate the value of this element—the prospect of a world to come—as a constituent of earthly happiness. I cannot but think that as the condition of mankind becomes improved, as they grow happier in their lives, and more capable of deriving happiness from unselfish sources, they will care less and less for this flattering expectation. It is not, naturally or generally, the happy who are the most anxious either for a prolongation of the present life, or for a life

hereafter : it is those who never have been happy.
They who have had their happiness can bear to part
with existence : but it is hard to die without ever
having lived. When mankind cease to need a future
existence as a consolation for the sufferings of the
present, it will have lost its chief value to them, for
themselves. I am now speaking of the unselfish.
Those who are so wrapped up in self that they are
unable to identify their feelings with anything which
will survive them, or to feel their life prolonged in
their younger cotemporaries and in all who help to
carry on the progressive movement of human affairs,
require the notion of another selfish life beyond the
grave, to enable them to keep up any interest in existence, since the present life, as its termination ap-
proaches, dwindles into something too insignificant to
be worth caring about. But if the Religion of
Humanity were as sedulously cultivated as the supernatural religions are (and there is no difficulty in
conceiving that it might be much more so), all who
had received the customary amount of moral cultivation would up to the hour of death live ideally in the
life of those who are to follow them : and though
doubtless they would often willingly survive as individuals for a much longer period than the present
duration of life, it appears to me probable that after a
length of time different in different persons, they
would have had enough of existence, and would

gladly lie down and take their eternal rest. Mean-
while and without looking so far forward, we may
remark, that those who believe the immortality of the
soul, generally quit life with fully as much, if not
more, reluctance, as those who have no such expectation. The mere cessation of existence is no evil to
any one: the idea is only formidable through the
illusion of imagination which makes one conceive
oneself as if one were alive and feeling oneself dead.
What is odious in death is not death itself, but the
act of dying, and its lugubrious accompaniments : all
of which must be equally undergone by the believer
in immortality. Nor can I perceive that the sceptic
loses by his scepticism any real and valuable consolation
except one ; the hope of reunion with those dear to
him who have ended their earthly life before him.
That loss, indeed, is neither to be denied nor extenu-
ated. In many cases it is beyond the reach of comparison or estimate; and will always suffice to keep
alive, in the more sensitive natures, the imaginative
hope of a futurity which, if there is nothing to prove,
there is as little in our knowledge and experience to
contradict.

History, so far as we know it, bears out the
opinion, that mankind can perfectly well do without
the belief in a heaven. The Greeks had anything
but a tempting idea of a future state. Their Elysian
fields held out very little attraction to their feelings

and imagination. Achilles in the Odyssey expressed a very natural, and no doubt a very common sentiment, when he said that he would rather be on earth the serf of a needy master, than reign over the whole kingdom of the dead. And the pensive character so striking in the address of the dying emperor Hadrian to his soul, gives evidence that the popular conception had not undergone much variation during that long interval. Yet we neither find that the Greeks enjoyed life less, nor feared death more, than other people. The Buddhist religion counts probably at this day a greater number of votaries than either the Christian or the Mahomedan. The Buddhist creed recognises many modes of punishment in a future life, or rather lives, by the transmigration of the soul into new bodies of men or animals. But the blessing from Heaven which it proposes as a reward, to be earned by perseverance in the highest order of virtuous life, is annihilation; the cessation, at least, of all conscious or separate existence. It is impossible to mistake in this religion, the work of legislators and moralists endeavouring to supply supernatural motives for the conduct which they were anxious to encourage; and they could find nothing more transcendant to hold out as the capital prize to be won by the mightiest efforts of labour and self-denial, than what we are so often told is the terrible idea of annihilation. Surely this is a proof that the idea is not really or naturally terrible ; that not philosophers only, but the common order of mankind, can easily reconcile themselves to it, and even consider it as a good; and that it is no un-natural part of the idea of a happy life, that life itself be laid down, after the best that it can give has been fully enjoyed through a long lapse of time ; when all its pleasures, even those of benevolence, are familiar, and nothing untasted and unknown is left to stimu-late curiosity and keep up the desire of prolonged existence.  It seems to me not only possible but pro-bable, that in a higher, and, above all, a happier con-dition of human life, not annihilation but immortality may be the burdensome idea; and that human nature, though pleased with the present, and by no means impatient to quit it, would find comfort and not sad-ness in the thought that it is not chained through eternity to a conscious existence which it cannot be assured that it will always wish to preserve.

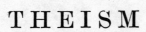

# THEISM

# THEISM

## PART I

### INTRODUCTION

THE contest which subsists from of old between
believers and unbelievers in natural and revealed
religion, has, like other permanent contests, varied
materially in its character from age to age; and the
present generation, at least in the higher regions of
controversy, shows, as compared with the 18th and
the beginning of the 19th century, a marked alteration in the aspect of the dispute. One feature of
this change is so apparent as to be generally acknowledged; the more softened temper in which the debate
is conducted on the part of unbelievers. The reac-
tionary violence, provoked by the intolerance of the
other side, has in a great measure exhausted itself.
Experience has abated the ardent hopes once entertained of the regeneration of the human race by
merely negative doctrine—by the destruction of
superstition. The philosophical study of history,

one of the most important creations of recent times,
has rendered possible an impartial estimate of the
doctrines and institutions of the past, from a relative
instead of an absolute point of view—as incidents of
human development at which it is useless to grumble,
and which may deserve admiration and gratitude for
their effects in the past, even though they may be
thought incapable of rendering similar services to the
future.  And the position assigned to Christianity
or Theism by the more instructed of those who reject
the supernatural, is that of things once of great value
but which can now be done without; rather than, as
formerly, of things misleading and noxious *ab initio.*

Along with this change in the moral attitude of
thoughtful unbelievers towards the religious ideas of
mankind, a corresponding difference has manifested
itself in their intellectual attitude.  The war against
religious beliefs, in the last century was carried on
principally on the ground of common sense or of
logic ; in the present age, on the ground of science.
The progress of the physical sciences is considered to
have established, by conclusive evidence, matters of
fact with which the religious traditions of mankind
are not reconcileable ; while the science of human
nature and history, is considered to show that the
creeds of the past are natural growths of the human
mind, in particular stages of its career, destined to
disappear and give place to other convictions in a

more advanced stage. In the progress of discussion this last class of considerations seems even to be superseding those which address themselves directly to the question of truth. Religions tend to be discussed, at least by those who reject them, less as intrinsically true or false than as products thrown up by certain states of civilization, and which, like the animal and vegetable productions of a geological period perish in those which succeed it from the cessation of the conditions necessary to their continued existence.

This tendency of recent speculation to look upon human opinions pre-eminently from an historical point of view, as facts obeying laws of their own, and requiring, like other observed facts, an historical or a scientific explanation (a tendency not confined to religious subjects), is by no means to be blamed, but to be applauded; not solely as drawing attention to an important and previously neglected aspect of human opinions, but because it has a real though indirect bearing upon the question of their truth. For, whatever opinion a person may adopt on any subject that admits of controversy, his assurance if he be a cautious thinker cannot be complete unless he is able to account for the existence of the opposite opinion. To ascribe it to the weakness of the human understanding is an explanation which cannot be sufficient for such a thinker, for he will

be slow to assume that he has himself a less share
of that infirmity than the rest of mankind and that
error is more likely to be on the other side than on
his own.    In his examination of evidence, the persuasion of others, perhaps of mankind in general,
is one of the data of the case—one of the phenomena to be accounted for.    As the human intellect
though weak is not essentially perverted, there is
a certain presumption of the truth of any opinion
held by many human minds, requiring to be rebutted
by assigning some other real or possible cause for
its prevalence.    And this consideration has a special
relevancy to the inquiry concerning the foundations
of theism, inasmuch as no argument for the truth
of theism is more commonly invoked or more confidently relied on, than the general assent of mankind.

But while giving its full value to this historical
treatment of the religious question, we ought not
therefore to let it supersede the dogmatic.    The most
important quality of an opinion on any momentous
subject is its truth or falsity, which to us resolves
itself into the sufficiency of the evidence on which it rests.
It is indispensable that the subject of religion should
from time to time be reviewed as a strictly scientific
question, and that its evidences should be tested by
the same scientific methods, and on the same principles
as those of any of the speculative conclusions drawn

by physical science.  It being granted then that the legitimate conclusions of science are entitled to prevail over all opinions, however widely held, which conflict with them,  and that the canons of scientific evidence which the successes and failures of two thousand years have established, are applicable to all subjects on which knowledge is attainable,  let us proceed to consider what place there is for religious beliefs on the platform of science ; what evidences they can appeal to, such as science can recognize, and what foundation there is for the doctrines of religion, considered as scientific theorems.

In this inquiry we of course begin with Natural Religion, the doctrine of the existence and attributes of God.

# THEISM

THOUGH I have defined the problem of Natural Theology, to be that of the existence of God or of a God, rather than of Gods, there is the amplest historical evidence that the belief in Gods is immeasurably more natural to the human mind than the belief in one author and ruler of nature; and that this more elevated belief is, compared with the former, an artificial product, requiring (except when impressed by early education) a considerable amount of intellectual culture before it can be reached. For a long time, the supposition appeared forced and unnatural that the diversity we see in the operations of nature can all be the work of a single will. To the untaught mind, and to all minds in pre-scientific times, the phenomena of nature seem to be the result of forces altogether heterogeneous, each taking its course quite independently of the others; and though to attribute them to conscious wills is eminently natural,

the natural tendency is to suppose as many such independent wills as there are distinguishable forces of
sufficient importance and interest to have been remarked and named.   There is no tendency in polytheism as such to transform itself spontaneously into
monotheism.   It is true that in polytheistic systems
generally the deity whose special attributes inspire
the greatest degree of awe, is usually supposed to
have a power of controlling the other deities; and
even in the most degraded perhaps of all such systems,
the Hindoo, adulation heaps upon the divinity who is
the immediate object of adoration, epithets like those
habitual to believers in a single God.   But there is
no real acknowledgment of one Governor.   Every
God normally rules his particular department though
there may be a still stronger God whose power when
he chooses to exert it can frustrate the purposes of the
inferior divinity.   There could be no real belief in one
Creator and Governor until mankind had begun to
see in the apparently confused phenomena which sur-
rounded them, a system capable of being viewed as
the possible working out of a single plan.   This conception of the world was perhaps anticipated (though
less frequently than is often supposed) by individuals of
exceptional genius, but it could only become common
after a rather long cultivation of scientific thought.

The special mode in which scientific study operates
to instil Monotheism in place of the more natural

Polytheism, is in no way mysterious. The specific
effect of science is to show by accumulating evidence,
that every event in nature is connected by laws with
some fact or facts which preceded it, or in other words,
depends for its existence on some antecedent; but yet
not so strictly on one, as not to be liable to frustration
or modification from others : for these distinct chains
of causation are so entangled with one another; the
action of each cause is so interfered with by other
causes, though each acts according to its own fixed
law; that every effect is truly the result rather of the
aggregate of all causes in existence than of any one
only; and nothing takes place in the world of our
experience without spreading a perceptible influence
of some sort through a greater or less portion of
Nature, and making perhaps every portion of it
slightly different from what it would have been if
that event had not taken place. Now, when once
the double conviction has found entry into the mind
—that every event depends on antecedents; and at
the same time that to bring it about many antecedents must concur, perhaps all the antecedents in
Nature, insomuch that a slight difference in any one
of them might have prevented the phenomenon, or
materially altered its character—the conviction follows
that no one event, certainly no one kind of events,
can be absolutely preordained or governed by any
Being but one who holds in his hand the reins of all

Nature and not of some department only. At least if a plurality be supposed, it is necessary to assume so complete a concert of action and unity of will among them that the difference is for most purposes immaterial between such a theory and that of the absolute unity of the Godhead.

The reason, then, why Monotheism may be accepted as the representative of Theism in the abstract, is not so much because it is the Theism of all the more improved portions of the human race, as because it is the only Theism which can claim for itself any footing on scientific ground. Every other theory of the government of the universe by supernatural beings, is inconsistent either with the carrying on of that government through a continual series of natural antecedents according to fixed laws, or with the interdependence of each of these series upon all the rest, which are the two most general results of science.

Setting out therefore from the scientific view of nature as one connected system, or united whole, united not like a web composed of separate threads in passive juxtaposition with one another, but rather like the human or animal frame, an apparatus kept going by perpetual action and reaction among all its parts ; it must be acknowledged that the question, to which Theism is an answer, is at least a very natural one, and issues from an obvious want of the human mind.

Accustomed as we are to find, in proportion to our means of observation, a definite beginning to each individual fact; and since wherever there is a beginning we find that there was an antecedent fact (called by us a cause), a fact but for which, the phenomenon which thus commences would not have been; it was impossible that the human mind should not ask itself whether the whole, of which these particular phenomena are a part, had not also a beginning, and if so, whether that beginning was not an origin; whether there was not something antecedent to the whole series of causes and effects that we term Nature, and but for which Nature itself would not have been. From the first recorded speculation this question has never remained without an hypothetical answer. The only answer which has long continued to afford satisfaction is Theism.

Looking at the problem, as it is our business to do, merely as a scientific inquiry, it resolves itself into two questions. First: Is the theory, which refers the origin of all the phenomena of nature to the will of a Creator, consistent or not with the ascertained results of science? Secondly, assuming it to be consistent, will its proofs bear to be tested by the principles of evidence and canons of belief by which our long experience of scientific inquiry has proved the necessity of being guided?

First, then: there is one conception of Theism

which is consistent, another which is radically inconsistent, with the most general truths that have been
made known to us by scientific investigation.

The one which is inconsistent is the conception of
a God governing the world by acts of variable will.
The one which is consistent, is the conception of a
God governing the world by invariable laws.

The primitive, and even in our own day the vulgar,
conception of the divine rule, is that the one God,
like the many Gods of antiquity, carries on the government of the world by special decrees, made *pro hac
vice*. Although supposed to be omniscient as well as
omnipotent, he is thought not to make up his mind
until the moment of action; or at least not so con-
clusively, but that his intentions may be altered up
to the very last moment by appropriate solicitation.
Without entering into the difficulties of reconciling
this view of the divine government with the pre-
science and the perfect wisdom ascribed to the Deity,
we may content ourselves with the fact that it con-
tradicts what experience has taught us of the manner
in which things actually take place. The phenomena
of Nature do take place according to general laws.
They do originate from definite natural antecedents.
Therefore if their ultimate origin is derived from a
will, that will must have established the general laws
and willed the antecedents. If there be a Creator,
his intention must have been that events should de-

pend upon antecedents and be produced according to fixed laws. But this being conceded, there is nothing in scientific experience inconsistent with the belief that those laws and sequences are themselves due to a divine will. Neither are we obliged to suppose that the divine will exerted itself once for all, and after putting a power into the system which enabled it to go on of itself, has ever since let it alone. Science contains nothing repugnant to the supposition that every event which takes place results from a specific volition of the presiding Power, provided that this Power adheres in its particular volitions to general laws laid down by itself. The common opinion is that this hypothesis tends more to the glory of the Deity than the supposition that the universe was made so that it could go on of itself. There have been thinkers however—of no ordinary eminence (of whom Leibnitz was one)—who thought the last the only supposition worthy of the Deity, and protested against likening God to a clockmaker whose clock will not go unless he puts his hand to the machinery and keeps it going. With such considerations we have no concern in this place. We are looking at the subject not from the point of view of reverence but from that of science; and with science both these suppositions as to the mode of the divine action are equally consistent.

We must now, however, pass to the next question.

There is nothing to disprove the creation and government of Nature by a sovereign will; but is there anything to prove it? Of what nature are its evidences; and weighed in the scientific balance, what is their value?

# THE EVIDENCES OF THEISM

THE evidences of a Creator are not only of several distinct kinds but of such diverse characters, that they are adapted to minds of very different descriptions, and it is hardly possible for any mind to be equally impressed by them all. The familiar classification of them into proofs *à priori* and *à posteriori*, marks that when looked at in a purely scientific view they belong to different schools of thought. Accordingly though the unthoughtful believer whose creed really rests on authority gives an equal welcome to all plausible arguments in support of the belief in which he has been brought up, philosophers who have had to make a choice between the *à priori* and the *à posteriori* methods in general science seldom fail, while insisting on one of these modes of support for religion, to speak with more or less of disparagement of the other. It is our duty in the present inquiry to maintain complete impartiality and to

give a fair examination to both.  At the same time
I entertain a strong conviction that one of the two
modes of argument is in its nature scientific, the
other not only unscientific but condemned by science.
The scientific argument is that which reasons from
the facts and analogies of human experience as a
geologist does when he infers the past states of our
terrestrial globe, or an astronomical observer when he
draws conclusions respecting the physical composition
of the heavenly bodies.  This is the *à posteriori*
method, the principal application of which to Theism
is the argument (as it is called) of design.  The mode
of reasoning which I call unscientific, though in the
opinion of some thinkers it is also a legitimate mode
of scientific procedure, is that which infers external
objective facts from ideas or convictions of our minds.
I say this independently of any opinion of my own
respecting the origin of our ideas or convictions; for
even if we were unable to point out any manner in
which the idea of God, for example, can have grown
up from the impressions of experience, still the idea
can only prove the idea, and not the objective fact,
unless indeed the fact is supposed (agreeably to the
book of Genesis) to have been handed down by tradition from a time when there was direct personal
intercourse with the Divine Being; in which case
the argument is no longer *à priori*.  The supposition
that an idea, or a wish, or a need, even if native to

the mind proves the reality of a corresponding object, derives all its plausibility from the belief already in our minds that we were made by a benignant Being who would not have implanted in us a groundless belief, or a want which he did not afford us the means of satisfying; and is therefore a palpable *petitio principii* if adduced as an argument to support the very belief which it presupposes.

At the same time, it must be admitted that all *à priori* systems whether in philosophy or religion, do, in some sense profess to be founded on experience, since though they affirm the possibility of arriving at truths which transcend experience, they yet make the facts of experience their starting point (as what other starting point is possible ?). They are entitled to consideration in so far as it can be shown that experience gives any countenance either to them or to their method of inquiry. Professedly *à priori* arguments are not unfrequently of a mixed nature, partaking in some degree of the *à posteriori* character, and may often be said to be *à posteriori* arguments in disguise; the *à priori* considerations acting chiefly in the way of making some particular *à posteriori* argument tell for more than its worth. This is emphatically true of the argument for Theism which I shall first examine, the necessity of a First Cause. For this has in truth a wide basis of experience in the universality of the relation of Cause and Effect among the phenomena of

nature; while at the same time, theological philosophers have not been content to let it rest upon this
basis, but have affirmed Causation as a truth of reason
apprehended intuitively by its own light.

# ARGUMENT FOR A FIRST CAUSE

THE argument for a First Cause admits of being, and is, presented as a conclusion from the whole of human experience. Everything that we know (it is argued) had a cause, and owed its existence to that cause. How then can it be but that the world, which is but a name for the aggregate of all that we know, has a cause to which it is indebted for its existence?

The fact of experience however, when correctly expressed, turns out to be, not that everything which we know derives its existence from a cause, but only every event or change. There is in Nature a permanent element, and also a changeable : the changes are always the effects of previous changes ; the permanent existences, so far as we know, are not effects at all. It is true we are accustomed to say not only of events, but of objects, that they are produced by causes, as water by the union of hydrogen and oxygen. But by this we only mean that when they begin to exist, their beginning is the effect of a cause. But their beginning to exist is not an object, it is an event. If it be objected that the cause of a thing's beginning to exist may be said with propriety to be the cause of the thing itself, I shall not quarrel with the expression. But that which in an object begins to exist, is that in it which belongs to the changeable element in nature; the outward form and the properties depending on mechanical or chemical combinations of its component parts. There is in every object another and a permanent element, viz., the specific elementary substance or substances of which it consists and their inherent properties. These are not known to us as beginning to exist : within the range of human knowledge they had no beginning, consequently no cause; though they themselves are causes or con-causes of everything that takes place. Experience therefore, affords no evidences, not even analogies, to justify our extending to the apparently immutable, a generalization grounded only on our observation of the changeable.

As a fact of experience, then, causation cannot legitimately be extended to the material universe itself, but only to its changeable phenomena; of these, indeed, causes may be affirmed without any exception. But what causes? The cause of every change is a prior change; and such it cannot but be; for if there were no new antecedent, there would not be a new consequent. If the state of facts which brings the phenomenon into existence, had existed always or for an indefinite duration, the effect also would have existed always or been produced an indefinite time ago. It is thus a necessary part of the fact of causation, within the sphere of our experience, that the causes as well as the effects had a beginning in time, and were themselves caused. It would seem therefore that our experience, instead of furnishing an argument for a first cause, is repugnant to it; and that the very essence of causation as it exists within the limits of our knowledge, is incompatible with a First Cause.

But it is necessary to look more particularly into the matter, and analyse more closely the nature of the causes of which mankind have experience. For if it should turn out that though all causes have a beginning, there is in all of them a permanent element which had no beginning, this permanent element may with some justice be termed a first or universal cause, inasmuch as though not sufficient of itself to cause anything, it enters as a con-cause into all causation. Now it happens that the last result of physical inquiry, derived from the converging evidences of all branches of physical science, does, if it holds good, land us so far as the material world is concerned, in a result of this sort. Whenever a physical phenomenon is traced to its cause, that cause when analysed is found to be a certain quantum of Force, combined with certain collocations. And the last great generalization of science, the Conservation of Force, teaches us that the variety in the effects depends partly upon the *amount* of the force, and partly upon the diversity of the collocations. The force itself is essentially one and the same; and there exists of it in nature a fixed quantity, which (if the theory be true) is never increased or diminished. Here then we find, even in the changes of material nature, a permanent element; to all appearance the very one of which we were in quest. This it is apparently to which if to anything we must assign the character of First Cause, the cause of the material universe. For all effects may be traced up to it, while it cannot be traced up, by our experience, to anything beyond: its transformations alone can be so traced, and of them the cause always includes the force itself: the same quantity of force, in some previous form. It would seem then that in the only sense in which experience supports in any shape the doctrine of a First Cause, viz., as the primæval and universal element in all causes, the First Cause can be no other than Force.

We are, however, by no means at the end of the question. On the contrary, the greatest stress of the argument is exactly at the point which we have now reached. For it is maintained that Mind is the only possible cause of Force; or rather perhaps, that Mind is a Force, and that all other force must be derived from it inasmuch as mind is the only thing which is capable of originating change. This is said to be the lesson of human experience. In the phenomena of inanimate nature the force which works is always a pre-existing force, not originated, but transferred. One physical object moves another by giving out to it the force by which it has first been itself moved. The wind communicates to the waves, or to a windmill, or a ship, part of the motion which has been given to itself by some other agent. In voluntary action alone we see a commencement, an origination of motion; since all other causes appear incapable of this origination experience is in favour of the conclusion that all the motion in existence owed its beginning to this one cause, voluntary agency, if not that of man, then of a more powerful Being.

This argument is a very old one. It is to be found in Plato; not as might have been expected, in the Phædon, where the arguments are not such as would now be deemed of any weight, but in his latest production, the Leges. And it is still one of the most telling arguments with the more metaphysical class of defenders of Natural Theology.

Now, in the first place, if there be truth in the

doctrine of the Conservation of Force, in other words the constancy of the total amount of Force in existence, this doctrine does not change from true to false when it reaches the field of voluntary agency. The will does not, any more than other causes, create Force: granting that it originates motion, it has no means of doing so but by converting into that particular manifestation a portion of Force which already existed in other forms. It is known that the source from which this portion of Force is derived, is chiefly, or entirely, the Force evolved in the processes of chemical composition and decomposition which constitute the body of nutrition: the force so liberated becomes a fund upon which every muscular and even every merely nervous action, as of the brain in thought, is a draft. It is in this sense only that, according to the best lights of science, volition is an originating cause. Volition, therefore, does not answer to the idea of a First Cause; since Force must in every instance be assumed as prior to it; and there is not the slightest colour, derived from experience, for supposing Force itself to have been created by a volition. As far as anything can be concluded from human experience Force has all the attributes of a thing eternal and uncreated.

This, however, does not close the discussion. For though whatever verdict experience can give in the

case is against the possibility that will ever originates
Force, yet if we can be assured that neither does Force
originate Will, Will must be held to be an agency, if
not prior to Force yet coeternal with it: and if it be
true that Will can originate, not indeed Force but the
transformation of Force from some other of its manifestations into that of mechanical motion, and that
there is within human experience no other agency
capable of doing so, the argument for a Will as the
originator, though not of the universe, yet of the
kosmos, or order of the universe, remains unanswered.

But the case thus stated is not conformable to fact.
Whatever volition can do in the way of creating
motion out of other forms of force, and generally of
evolving force from a latent into a visible state, can
be done by many other causes. Chemical action, for
instance; electricity; heat; the mere presence of a
gravitating body; all these are causes of mechanical
motion on a far larger scale than any volitions which
experience presents to us: and in most of the effects
thus produced the motion given by one body to another,
is not, as in the ordinary cases of mechanical action,
motion that has first been given to that other by some
third body. The phenomenon is not a mere passing
on of mechanical motion, but a creation of it out of a
force previously latent or manifesting itself in some
other form. Volition, therefore, regarded as an agent
in the material universe, has no exclusive privilege of

origination : all that it can originate is also originated
by other transforming agents.  If it be said that those
other agents must have had the force they give out
put into them from elsewhere, I answer, that this is
no less true of the force which volition disposes of.
We know that this force comes from an external source,
the chemical action of the food and air.  The force by
which the phenomena of the material world are produced, circulates through all physical agencies in a never
ending though sometimes intermitting stream.  I am,
of course, speaking of volition only in its action on
the material world.  We have nothing to do here
with the freedom of the will itself as a mental phenomenon—with the *vexata questio* whether volition is
self-determining or determined by causes.  To the
question now in hand it is only the effects of volition
that are relevant, not its origin.  The assertion is that
physical nature must have been produced by a Will,
because nothing but Will is known to us as having
the power of originating the production of phenomena.
We have seen that, on the contrary, all the power
that Will possesses over phenomena is shared, as far
as we have the means of judging, by other and much
more powerful agents, and that in the only sense in
which those agents do not originate, neither does
Will originate.  No prerogative, therefore, can, on the
ground of experience, be assigned to volition above
other natural agents, as a producing cause of pheno-

mena. All that can be affirmed by the strongest assertor of the Freedom of the Will, is that volitions are themselves uncaused and are therefore alone fit to be the first or universal Cause. But, even assuming volitions to be uncaused, the properties of matter, so far as experience discloses, are uncaused also, and have the advantage over any particular volition, in being so far as experience can show, eternal. Theism, therefore, in so far as it rests on the necessity of a First Cause, has no support from experience.

To those who, in default of Experience, consider the necessity of a first cause as matter of intuition, I would say that it is needless, in this discussion, to contest their premises; since admitting that there is and must be a First Cause, it has now been shown that several other agencies than Will can lay equal claim to that character. One thing only may be said which requires notice here. Among the facts of the universe to be accounted for, it may be said, is Mind; and it is self-evident that nothing can have produced Mind but Mind.

The special indications that Mind is deemed to give, pointing to intelligent contrivance, belong to a different portion of this inquiry. But if the mere existence of Mind is supposed to require, as a necessary antecedent, another Mind greater and more powerful, the difficulty is not removed by going one step back : the creating mind stands as much in need of another mind to be the source of its existence, as the created mind. Be it remembered that we have no direct knowledge (at least apart from Revelation) of a Mind which is even apparently eternal, as Force and Matter are : an eternal mind is, as far as the present argument is concerned, a simple hypothesis to account for the minds which we know to exist. Now it is essential to an hypothesis that if admitted it should at least remove the difficulty and account for the facts. But it does not account for Mind to refer one mind to a prior mind for its origin. The problem remains unsolved, the difficulty undiminished, nay, rather increased.

To this it may be objected that the causation of every human mind is matter of fact, since we know that it had a beginning in time. We even know, or have the strongest grounds for believing that the human species itself had a beginning in time. For there is a vast amount of evidence that the state of our planet was once such as to be incompatible with animal life, and that human life is of very much more modern origin than animal life. In any case, therefore, the fact must be faced that there must have been a cause which called the first human mind, nay the very first germ of organic life, into existence. No such difficulty exists in the supposition of an Eternal Mind. If we did not know that Mind on our earth began to exist, we might suppose it to be uncaused ;

and we may still suppose this of the mind to which
we ascribe its existence.

To take this ground is to return into the field of
human experience, and to become subject to its canons,
and we are then entitled to ask where is the proof
that nothing can have caused a mind except another
mind. From what, except from experience, can we
know what can produce what—what causes are
adequate to what effects? That nothing can
*consciously* produce Mind but Mind, is self-evident,
being involved in the meaning of the words; but
that there cannot be unconscious production must
not be assumed, for it is the very point to be proved.
Apart from experience, and arguing on what is
called reason, that is on supposed self-evidence, the
notion seems to be, that no causes can give rise to
products of a more precious or elevated kind than
themselves. But this is at variance with the known
analogies of Nature. How vastly nobler and more
precious, for instance, are the higher vegetables and
animals than the soil and manure out of which, and
by the properties of which they are raised up! The
tendency of all recent speculation is towards the
opinion that the development of inferior orders of
existence into superior, the substitution of greater
elaboration and higher organization for lower, is the
general rule of Nature. Whether it is so or not,
there are at least in Nature a multitude of facts bear-

ing that character, and this is sufficient for the argument.

Here, then, this part of the discussion may stop. The result it leads to is that the First Cause argument is in itself of no value for the establishment of Theism : because no cause is needed for the existence of that which has no beginning; and both Matter and Force (whatever metaphysical theory we may give of the one or the other) have had, so far as our experience can teach us, no beginning—which cannot be said of Mind. The phenomena or changes in the universe have indeed each of them a beginning and a cause, but their cause is always a prior change ; nor do the analogies of experience give us any reason to expect, from the mere occurrence of changes, that if we could trace back the series far enough we should arrive at a Primæval Volition. The world does not, by its mere existence, bear witness to a God: if it gives indications of one, these must be given by the special nature of the phenomena, by what they present that resembles adaptation to an end : of which hereafter. If, in default of evidence from experience, the evidence of intuition is relied upon, it may be answered that if Mind, as Mind, presents intuitive evidence of having been created, the Creative Mind must do the same, and we are no nearer to the First Cause than before. But if there be nothing in the nature of mind which in itself implies a Creator, the minds which have a beginning in time, as all minds have which are known to our experience, must indeed have been caused, but it is not necessary that their cause should have been a prior Intelligence.

# ARGUMENT FROM THE GENERAL CONSENT OF MANKIND

BEFORE proceeding to the argument from Marks of Design, which, as it seems to me, must always be the main strength of Natural Theism, we may dispose briefly of some other arguments which are of little scientific weight but which have greater influence on the human mind than much better arguments, because they are appeals to authority, and it is by authority that the opinions of the bulk of mankind are principally and not unnaturally governed. The authority invoked is that of mankind generally, and specially of some of its wisest men; particularly such as were in other respects conspicuous examples of breaking loose from received prejudices. Socrates and Plato, Bacon, Locke, and Newton, Descartes and Leibnitz, are common examples.

It may doubtless be good advice to persons who in point of knowledge and cultivation are not entitled to think themselves competent judges of difficult questions, to bid them content themselves with holding that true which mankind generally believe, and so long as they believe it; or that which has been believed by those who pass for the most eminent among the minds of the past. But to a thinker the argument from other people's opinions has little weight. It is but second-hand evidence; and merely admonishes us to look out for and weigh the reasons on which this conviction of mankind or of wise men was founded. Accordingly, those who make any claim to philosophic treatment of the subject, employ this general consent chiefly as evidence that there is in the mind of man an intuitive perception, or an instinctive sense, of Deity. From the generality of the belief, they infer that it is inherent in our constitution; from which they draw the conclusion, a precarious one indeed, but conformable to the general mode of proceeding of the intuitive philosophy, that the belief must be true; though as applied to Theism this argument begs the question, since it has itself nothing to rest upon but the belief that the human mind was made by a God, who would not deceive his creatures.

But, indeed, what ground does the general prevalence of the belief in Deity afford us for inferring that this belief is native to the human mind, and independent of evidence? Is it then so very devoid of evidence, even apparent? Has it so little semblance of foundation in fact, that it can only be ac-

counted for by the supposition of its being innate?
We should not expect to find Theists believing that
the appearances in Nature of a contriving Intelligence
are not only insufficient but are not even plausible,
and cannot be supposed to have carried conviction
either to the general or to the wiser mind.  If there
are external evidences of theism, even if not perfectly
conclusive, why need we suppose that the belief of
its truth was the result of anything else?  The
superior minds to whom an appeal is made, from
Socrates downwards, when they professed to give the
grounds of their opinion, did not say that they found
the belief in themselves without knowing from whence
it came, but ascribed it, if not to revelation, either
to some metaphysical argument, or to those very
external evidences which are the basis of the argument from Design.

If it be said that the belief in Deity is universal
among barbarous tribes, and among the ignorant portion of civilized populations, who cannot be supposed
to have been impressed by the marvellous adaptations
of Nature most of which are unknown to them; I
answer, that the ignorant in civilized countries take
their opinions from the educated, and that in the
case of savages, if the evidence is insufficient, so is
the belief.  The religious belief of savages is not belief in the God of Natural Theology, but a mere modification of the crude generalization which ascribes

life, consciousness and will to all natural powers of
which they cannot perceive the source or control the
operation. And the divinities believed in are as
numerous as those powers. Each river, fountain or
tree has a divinity of its own. To see in this blunder
of primitive ignorance the hand of the Supreme
Being implanting in his creatures an instinctive
knowledge of his existence, is a poor compliment to
the Deity. The religion of savages is Fetichism of
the grossest kind, ascribing animation and will to
individual objects, and seeking to propitiate them by
prayer and sacrifice. That this should be the case is
the less surprising when we remember that there is
not a definite boundary line, broadly separating the
conscious human being from inanimate objects. Between these and man there is an intermediate class of
objects, sometimes much more powerful than man,
which do possess life and will, viz. the brute animals,
which in an early stage of existence play a very great
part in human life; making it the less surprising that
the line should not at first be quite distinguishable between the animate and the inanimate part of Nature.
As observation advances, it is perceived that the
majority of outward objects have all their important
qualities in common with entire classes or groups of
objects which comport themselves exactly alike in the
same circumstances, and in these cases the worship of
visible objects is exchanged for that of an invisible

Being supposed to preside over the whole class.   This step in generalization is slowly made, with hesitation and even terror; as we still see in the case of ignorant populations with what difficulty experience disabuses them of belief in the supernatural powers and terrible resentment of a particular idol.   Chiefly by these terrors the religious impressions of barbarians are kept alive, with only slight modifications, until the Theism of cultivated minds is ready to take their place.   And the Theism of cultivated minds, if we take their own word for it, is always a conclusion either from arguments called rational, or from the appearances in Nature.

It is needless here to dwell upon the difficulty of the hypothesis of a natural belief not common to all human beings, an instinct not universal.   It is conceivable, doubtless, that some men might be born without a particular natural faculty, as some are born without a particular sense.   But when this is the case we ought to be much more particular as to the proof that it really is a natural faculty.   If it were not a matter of observation but of speculation that men can see; if they had no apparent organ of sight, and no perceptions or knowledge but such as they might conceivably have acquired by some circuitous process through their other senses, the fact that men exist who do not even suppose themselves to see, would be a considerable argument against the theory of a visual sense. But it would carry us too far to press, for the purposes of this discussion, an argument which applies so largely to the whole of the intuitional philosophy. The strongest Intuitionist will not maintain that a belief should be held for instinctive when evidence (real or apparent), sufficient to engender it, is universally admitted to exist. To the force of the evidence must be, in this case, added all the emotional or moral causes which incline men to the belief; the satisfaction which it gives to the obstinate questionings with which men torment themselves respecting the past; the hopes which it opens for the future; the fears also, since fear as well as hope predisposes to belief; and to these in the case of the more active spirits must always have been added a perception of the power which belief in the supernatural affords for governing mankind, either for their own good, or for the selfish purposes of the governors.

The general consent of mankind does not, therefore, afford ground for admitting, even as an hypothesis, the origin in an inherent law of the human mind, of a fact otherwise so more than sufficiently, so amply, accounted for.

# THE ARGUMENT FROM CONSCIOUSNESS

THERE have been numerous arguments, indeed almost every religious metaphysician has one of his own, to prove the existence and attributes of God from what are called truths of reason, supposed to be independent of experience. Descartes, who is the real founder of the intuitional metaphysics, draws the conclusion immediately from the first premise of his philosophy, the celebrated assumption that whatever he could very clearly and distinctly apprehend, must be true. The idea of a God, perfect in power, wisdom, and goodness, is a clear and distinct idea, and must therefore, on this principle correspond to a real object. This bold generalization, however, that a conception of the human mind proves its own objective reality, Descartes is obliged to limit by the qualification—" if the idea includes existence." Now the idea of God implying the union of all perfections, and existence being a perfection, the idea of God proves his existence. This very simple argument, which denies to man one of his most familiar and most precious attributes, that of idealizing as it is called—of constructing from the materials of experience a conception more perfect than experience itself affords—is not likely to satisfy any one in the present day. More elaborate, though scarcely more successful efforts, have been made by many of Descartes' successors, to derive knowledge of the Deity from an inward light: to make it a truth not dependent on external evidence, a fact of direct perception, or, as they are accustomed to call it, of consciousness. The philosophical world is familiar with the attempt of Cousin to make out that whenever we perceive a particular object, we perceive along with it, or are conscious of, God; and also with the celebrated refutation of this doctrine by Sir William Hamilton. It would be waste of time to examine any of these theories in detail. While each has its own particular logical fallacies, they labour under the common infirmity, that one man cannot by proclaiming with ever so much confidence that *he* perceives an object, convince other people that they see it too. If, indeed, he laid claim to a divine faculty of vision, vouchsafed to him alone, and making him cognizant of things which men not thus assisted have not the capacity to see, the case might be different. Men have been able to get such

claims admitted; and other people can only require
of them to show their credentials. But when no
claim is set up to any peculiar gift, but we are told
that all of us are as capable as the prophet of seeing
what he sees, feeling what he feels, nay, that we
actually do so, and when the utmost effort of which
we are capable fails to make us aware of what we are
told we perceive, this supposed universal faculty of
intuition is but

> " The dark lantern of the Spirit
> Which none see by but those who bear it :"

and the bearers may fairly be asked to consider
whether it is not more likely that they are mistaken
as to the origin of an impression in their minds, than
that others are ignorant of the very existence of an
impression in theirs.

The inconclusiveness, in a speculative point of
view, of all arguments from the subjective notion of
Deity to its objective reality, was well seen by
Kant, the most discriminating of the *à priori*
metaphysicians, who always kept the two questions,
the origin and composition of our ideas, and the
reality of the corresponding objects, perfectly distinct. According to Kant the idea of the Deity
is native to the mind, in the sense that it is constructed by the mind's own laws and not derived
from without: but this Idea of Speculative Reason
cannot be shown by any logical process or perceived

by direct apprehension, to have a corresponding
Reality outside the human mind. To Kant, God
is neither an object of direct consciousness nor a
conclusion of reasoning, but a Necessary Assumption; necessary, not by a logical, but a practical
necessity, imposed by the reality of the Moral Law.
Duty is a fact of consciousness: "Thou shalt" is
a command issuing from the recesses of our being,
and not to be accounted for by any impressions
derived from experience; and this command requires
a commander, though it is not perfectly clear
whether Kant's meaning is that conviction of a law
includes conviction of a lawgiver, or only that a
Being of whose will the law is an expression, is
eminently desirable. If the former be intended,
the argument is founded on a double meaning of
the word Law. A rule to which we feel it a duty
to conform has in common with laws commonly
so called, the fact of claiming our obedience; but
it does not follow that the rule must originate,
like the laws of the land, in the will of a legislator
or legislators external to the mind. We may even
say that a feeling of obligation which is merely
the result of a command is not what is meant by
moral obligation, which, on the contrary, supposes
something that the internal conscience bears witness
to as binding in its own nature; and which God,
in superadding his command, conforms to and per-

haps declares, but does not create.  Conceding, then,
for the sake of the argument, that the moral sentiment is as purely of the mind's own growth,
the obligation of duty as entirely independent of
experience and acquired impressions, as Kant or
any other metaphysician ever contended, it may yet
be maintained that this feeling of obligation rather
excludes, than compels, the belief in a Divine legislator merely as the source of the obligation: and
as a matter of fact, the obligation of duty is both
theoretically acknowledged and practically felt in the
fullest manner by many who have no positive belief
in God, though seldom, probably, without habitual
and familiar reference to him as an ideal conception.
But if the existence of God as a wise and just
lawgiver, is not a necessary part of the feelings of
morality, it may still be maintained that those feelings
make his existence eminently desirable.  No doubt
they do, and that is the great reason why we
find that good men and women cling to the belief,
and are pained by its being questioned.  But surely
it is not legitimate to assume that in the order
of the Universe, whatever is desirable is true.  Optimism, even when a God is already believed in, is
a thorny doctrine to maintain, and had to be taken
by Leibnitz in the limited sense, that the universe
being made by a good being, is the best universe
possible, not the best absolutely: that the Divine

power, in short, was not equal to making it more free from imperfections than it is. But optimism prior to belief in a God, and as the ground of that belief, seems one of the oddest of all speculative delusions. Nothing, however, I believe, contributes more to keep up the belief in the general mind of humanity than this feeling of its desirableness, which, when clothed, as it very often is, in the forms of an argument, is a *naïf* expression of the tendency of the human mind to believe what is agreeable to it. Positive value the argument of course has none.

Without dwelling further on these or on any other of the *à priori* arguments for Theism, we will no longer delay passing to the far more important argument of the appearances of Contrivance in Nature.

# THE ARGUMENT FROM MARKS OF DESIGN IN NATURE

WE now at last reach an argument of a really scientific character, which does not shrink from scientific tests, but claims to be judged by the established canons of Induction. The Design argument is wholly grounded on experience. Certain qualities, it is alleged, are found to be characteristic of such things as are made by an intelligent mind for a purpose. The order of Nature, or some considerable parts of it, exhibit these qualities in a remarkable degree. We are entitled, from this great similarity in the effects, to infer similarity in the cause, and to believe that things which it is beyond the power of man to make, but which resemble the works of man in all but power, must also have been made by Intelligence, armed with a power greater than human.

I have stated this argument in its fullest strength, as it is stated by its most thoroughgoing assertors.

A very little consideration, however, suffices to show that though it has some force, its force is very generally overrated. Paley's illustration of a watch puts the case much too strongly. If I found a watch on an apparently desolate island, I should indeed infer that it had been left there by a human being; but the inference would not be from marks of design, but because I already knew by direct experience that watches are made by men. I should draw the inference no less confidently from a foot print, or from any relic however insignificant which experience has taught me to attribute to man : as geologists infer the past existence of animals from coprolites, though no one sees marks of design in a coprolite. The evidence of design in creation can never reach the height of direct induction; it amounts only to the inferior kind of inductive evidence called analogy. Analogy agrees with induction in this, that they both argue that a thing known to resemble another in certain circumstances (call those circumstances A and B) will resemble it in another circumstance (call it C). But the difference is that in induction, A and B are known, by a previous comparison of many instances, to be the very circumstances on which C depends, or with which it is in some way connected. When this has not been ascertained, the argument amounts only to this, that since it is not known with which of the circumstances existing in the known case C is connected, they may as well be A and B as any others; and therefore there is a greater probability of C in cases where we know that A and B exist, than in cases of which we know nothing at all. This argument is of a weight very difficult to estimate at all, and impossible to estimate precisely. It may be very strong, when the known points of agreement, A and B &c. are numerous and the known points of difference few; or very weak, when the reverse is the case: but it can never be equal in validity to a real induction. The resemblances between some of the arrangements in nature and some of those made by man are considerable, and even as mere resemblances afford a certain presumption of similarity of cause: but how great that presumption is, it is hard to say. All that can be said with certainty is that these likenesses make creation by intelligence considerably more probable than if the likenesses had been less, or than if there had been no likenesses at all.

This mode, however, of stating the case does not do full justice to the evidence of Theism. The Design argument is not drawn from mere resemblances in Nature to the works of human intelligence, but from the special character of those resemblances. The circumstances in which it is alleged that the world resembles the works of man are not circumstances taken at random, but are particular instances of a circumstance which experience shows to have a real connection with an intelligent origin, the fact of conspiring to an end. The argument therefore is not one of mere analogy. As mere analogy it has its weight, but it is more than analogy. It surpasses analogy exactly as induction surpasses it. It is an inductive argument.

This, I think, is undeniable, and it remains to test the argument by the logical principles applicable to Induction. For this purpose it will be convenient to handle, not the argument as a whole, but some one of the most impressive cases of it, such as the structure of the eye, or of the ear. It is maintained that the structure of the eye proves a designing mind. To what class of inductive arguments does this belong? and what is its degree of force?

The species of inductive arguments are four in number, corresponding to the four Inductive Methods; the Methods of Agreement, of Difference, of Residues, and of Concomitant Variations. The argument under consideration falls within the first of these divisions, the Method of Agreement. This is, for reasons known to inductive logicians, the weakest of the four, but the particular argument is a strong one of the kind. It may be logically analysed as follows:

The parts of which the eye is composed, and the collocations which constitute the arrangement of those parts, resemble one another in this very remarkable property, that they all conduce to enabling the animal

to see. These things being as they are, the animal
sees : if any one of them were different from what it is,
the animal, for the most part, would either not see, or
would not see equally well. And this is the only
marked resemblance that we can trace among the different parts of this structure, beyond the general
likeness of composition and organization which exists
among all other parts of the animal. Now the particular combination of organic elements called an eye had,
in every instance, a beginning in time and must therefore have been brought together by a cause or causes.
The number of instances is immeasurably greater
than is, by the principles of inductive logic, required
for the exclusion of a random concurrence of independent causes, or speaking technically, for the elimi-
nation of chance. We are therefore warranted by the
canons of induction in concluding that what brought
all these elements together was some cause common to
them all; and inasmuch as the elements agree in the
single circumstance of conspiring to produce sight,
there must be some connection by way of causation
between the cause which brought those elements
together, and the fact of sight.

This I conceive to be a legitimate inductive inference, and the sum and substance of what Induction
can do for Theism. The natural sequel of the argument would be this. Sight, being a fact not precedent
but subsequent to the putting together of the organic

structure of the eye, can only be connected with the production of that structure in the character of a final, not an efficient cause; that is, it is not Sight itself but an antecedent Idea of it, that must be the efficient cause. But this at once marks the origin as proceeding from an intelligent will.

I regret to say, however, that this latter half of the argument is not so inexpugnable as the former half. Creative forethought is not absolutely the only link by which the origin of the wonderful mechanism of the eye may be connected with the fact of sight. There is another connecting link on which attention has been greatly fixed by recent speculations, and the reality of which cannot be called in question, though its adequacy to account for such truly admirable combinations as some of those in Nature, is still and will probably long remain problematical. This is the principle of "the survival of the fittest."

This principle does not pretend to account for the commencement of sensation or of animal or vegetable life. But assuming the existence of some one or more very low forms of organic life, in which there are no complex adaptations nor any marked appearances of contrivance, and supposing, as experience warrants us in doing, that many small variations from those simple types would be thrown out in all directions, which would be transmissible by inheritance, and of which some would be advantageous to the creature in its struggle

for existence and others disadvantageous, the forms
which are advantageous would always tend to survive
and those which are disadvantageous to perish. And
thus there would be a constant though slow general
improvement of the type as it branched out into
many different varieties, adapting it to different media
and modes of existence, until it might possibly, in
countless ages, attain to the most advanced examples
which now exist.

It must be acknowledged that there is something
very startling, and *prima facie* improbable in this
hypothetical history of Nature. It would require us,
for example, to suppose that the primæval animal of
whatever nature it may have been, could not see, and
had at most such slight preparation for seeing as
might be constituted by some chemical action of
light upon its cellular structure. One of the accidental variations which are liable to take place in
all organic beings would at some time or other produce a variety that could see, in some imperfect manner, and this peculiarity being transmitted by inheritance, while other variations continued to take place in
other directions, a number of races would be produced
who, by the power of even imperfect sight, would
have a great advantage over all other creatures which
could not see and would in time extirpate them from
all places, except, perhaps, a few very peculiar situ-
ations underground. Fresh variations supervening

would give rise to races with better and better seeing powers until we might at last reach as extraordinary a combination of structures and functions as are seen in the eye of man and of the more important animals. Of this theory when pushed to this extreme point, all that can now be said is that it is not so absurd as it looks, and that the analogies which have been discovered in experience, favourable to its possibility, far exceed what any one could have supposed beforehand. Whether it will ever be possible to say more than this, is at present uncertain. The theory if admitted would be in no way whatever inconsistent with Creation. But it must be acknowledged that it would greatly attenuate the evidence for it.

Leaving this remarkable speculation to whatever fate the progress of discovery may have in store for it, I think it must be allowed that, in the present state of our knowledge, the adaptations in Nature afford a large balance of probability in favour of creation by intelligence. It is equally certain that this is no more than a probability; and that the various other arguments of Natural Theology which we have considered, add nothing to its force. Whatever ground there is, revelation apart, to believe in an Author of Nature, is derived from the appearances in the universe. Their mere resemblance to the works of man, or to what man could do if he had the same power over the materials of organized bodies which

he has over the materials of a watch, is of some value
as an argument of analogy: but the argument is
greatly strengthened by the properly inductive considerations which establish that there is some connection through causation between the origin of the
arrangements of nature and the ends they fulfil; an
argument which is in many cases slight, but in others,
and chiefly in the nice and intricate combinations of
vegetable and animal life, is of considerable strength.

# PART II

## ATTRIBUTES

THE question of the existence of a Deity, in its purely scientific aspect, standing as is shown in the First Part, it is next to be considered, given the indications of a Deity, what *sort* of a Deity do they point to? What attributes are we warranted, by the evidence which Nature affords of a creative mind, in assigning to that mind?

It needs no showing that the power if not the intelligence, must be so far superior to that of Man, as to surpass all human estimate. But from this to Omnipotence and Omniscience there is a wide interval. And the distinction is of immense practical importance.

It is not too much to say that every indication of Design in the Kosmos is so much evidence against the Omnipotence of the Designer. For what is meant by Design? Contrivance: the adaptation of means to an end. But the necessity for contrivance—the need of employing means—is a consequence of the limitation of power. Who would have recourse to means if to attain his end his mere word was sufficient? The very idea of means implies that the means have an efficacy which the direct action of the being who employs them has not. Otherwise they are not means, but an incumbrance. A man does not use machinery to move his arms. If he did, it could only be when paralysis had deprived him of the power of moving them by volition. But if the employment of contrivance is in itself a sign of limited power, how much more so is the careful and skilful choice of contrivances? Can any wisdom be shown in the selection of means, when the means have no efficacy but what is given them by the will of him who employs them, and when his will could have bestowed the same efficacy on any other means? Wisdom and contrivance are shown in overcoming difficulties, and there is no room for them in a Being for whom no difficulties exist. The evidences, therefore, of Natural Theology distinctly imply that the author of the Kosmos worked under limitations; that he was obliged to adapt himself to conditions independent of his will, and to attain his ends by such arrangements as those conditions admitted of.

And this hypothesis agrees with what we have seen to be the tendency of the evidences in another respect. We found that the appearances in Nature point indeed to an origin of the Kosmos, or order in Nature, and indicate that origin to be Design but do not point to any commencement, still less creation, of the two great elements of the Universe, the passive element and the active element, Matter and Force. There is in Nature no reason whatever to suppose that either Matter or Force, or any of their properties, were made by the Being who was the author of the collocations by which the world is adapted to what we consider as its purposes; or that he has power to alter any of those properties. It is only when we consent to entertain this negative supposition that there arises a need for wisdom and contrivance in the order of the universe. The Deity had on this hypothesis to work out his ends by combining materials of a given nature and properties. Out of these materials he had to construct a world in which his designs should be carried into effect through given properties of Matter and Force, working together and fitting into one another. This did require skill and contrivance, and the means by which it is effected are often such as justly excite our wonder and admiration : but exactly because it requires wisdom, it implies limitation of power, or rather the two phrases express different sides of the same fact.

If it be said, that an Omnipotent Creator, though under no necessity of employing contrivances such as man must use, thought fit to do so in order to leave traces by which man might recognize his creative hand, the answer is that this equally supposes a limit to his omnipotence. For if it was his will that men should know that they themselves and the world are his work, he, being omnipotent, had only to will that they should be aware of it. Ingenious men have sought for reasons why God might choose to leave his existence so far a matter of doubt that men should not be under an absolute necessity of knowing it, as they are of knowing that three and two make five. These imagined reasons are very unfortunate specimens of casuistry ; but even did we admit their validity, they are of no avail on the supposition of omnipotence, since if it did not please God to implant in man a complete conviction of his exist- ence, nothing hindered him from making the convic- tion fall short of completeness by any margin he chose to leave. It is usual to dispose of arguments of this description by the easy answer, that we do not know what wise reasons the Omniscient may have had for leaving undone things which he had the power to do. It is not perceived that this plea itself implies a limit to Omnipotence. When a thing is obviously good and obviously in accordance with what all the evidences of creation imply to have been the Creator's design, and we say we do not know what good reason he may have had for not doing it, we mean that we do not know to what other, still better object—to what object still more completely in the line of his purposes, he may have seen fit to postpone it. But the necessity of postponing one thing to another belongs only to limited power. Omnipotence could have made the objects compatible. Omnipotence does not need to weigh one consideration against another. If the Creator, like a human ruler, had to adapt himself to a set of conditions which he did not make, it is as unphilosophical as presumptuous in us to call him to account for any imperfections in his work; to complain that he left anything in it contrary to what, if the indications of design prove anything, he must have intended. He must at least know more than we know, and we cannot judge what greater good would have had to be sacrificed, or what greater evil incurred, if he had decided to remove this particular blot. Not so if he be omnipotent. If he be that, he must himself have willed that the two desirable objects should be incompatible; he must himself have willed that the obstacle to his supposed design should be insuperable. It cannot therefore *be* his design. It will not do to say that it was, but that he had other designs which interfered with it; for no one purpose imposes necessary limitations on another in the case of a Being not restricted by conditions of possibility.

Omnipotence, therefore, cannot be predicated of the Creator on grounds of natural theology. The fundamental principles of natural religion as deduced

from the facts of the universe, negative his omnipotence. They do not, in the same manner, exclude
omniscience: if we suppose limitation of power,
there is nothing to contradict the supposition of
perfect knowledge and absolute wisdom. But neither
is there anything to prove it. The knowledge of
the powers and properties of things necessary for
planning and executing the arrangements of the
Kosmos, is no doubt as much in excess of human
knowledge as the power implied in creation is in
excess of human power. And the skill, the subtlety
of contrivance, the ingenuity as it would be called
in the case of a human work, is often marvellous.
But nothing obliges us to suppose that either the
knowledge or the skill is infinite. We are not even
compelled to suppose that the contrivances were
always the best possible. If we venture to judge
them as we judge the works of human artificers, we
find abundant defects. The human body, for example, is one of the most striking instances of artful
and ingenious contrivance which nature offers, but
we may well ask whether so complicated a machine
could not have been made to last longer, and not
to get so easily and frequently out of order. We
may ask why the human race should have been so
constituted as to grovel in wretchedness and degra-
dation for countless ages before a small portion of
it was enabled to lift itself into the very imperfect

state of intelligence, goodness and happiness which
we enjoy. The divine power may not have been
equal to doing more; the obstacles to a better arrangement of things may have been insuperable.
But it is also possible that they were not. The skill
of the Demiourgos was sufficient to produce what
we see; but we cannot tell that this skill reached
the extreme limit of perfection compatible with the
material it employed and the forces it had to work
with. I know not how we can even satisfy ourselves
on grounds of natural theology, that the Creator
foresees all the future; that he foreknows all the
effects that will issue from his own contrivances.
There may be great wisdom without the power of
foreseeing and calculating everything: and human
workmanship teaches us the possibility that the
workman's knowledge of the properties of the things
he works on may enable him to make arrangements
admirably fitted to produce a given result, while he
may have very little power of foreseeing the agencies
of another kind which may modify or counteract
the operation of the machinery he has made. Perhaps a knowledge of the laws of nature on which
organic life depends, not much more perfect than
the knowledge which man even now possesses of
some other natural laws, would enable man, if he
had the same power over the materials and the forces
concerned which he has over some of those of

inanimate nature, to create organized beings not less wonderful nor less adapted to their conditions of existence than those in Nature.

Assuming then that while we confine ourselves to Natural Religion we must rest content with a Creator less than Almighty; the question presents itself, of what nature is the limitation of his power? Does the obstacle at which the power of the Creator stops, which says to it: Thus far shalt thou go and no further, lie in the power of other Intelligent Beings; or in the insufficiency and refractoriness of the materials of the universe; or must we resign ourselves to admitting the hypothesis that the author of the Kosmos, though wise and knowing, was not all-wise and all-knowing, and may not always have done the best that was possible under the conditions of the problem?

The first of these suppositions has until a very recent period been and in many quarters still is, the prevalent theory even of Christianity. Though attributing, and in a certain sense sincerely, omnipotence to the Creator, the received religion represents him as for some inscrutable reason tolerating the perpetual counteraction of his purposes by the will of another Being of opposite character and of great though inferior power, the Devil. The only difference on this matter between popular Christianity and the religion of Ormuzd and Ahriman, is that the former pays its good Creator the bad compliment of having been the maker of the Devil and of being at all times able to crush and annihilate him and his evil deeds and counsels, which nevertheless he does not do. But, as I have already remarked, all forms of polytheism, and this among the rest, are with difficulty reconcileable with an universe governed by general laws. Obedience to law is the note of a settled government, and not of a conflict always going on. When powers are at war with one another for the rule of the world, the boundary between them is not fixed but constantly fluctuating. This may seem to be the case on our planet as between the powers of good and evil when we look only at the results; but when we consider the inner springs, we find that both the good and the evil take place in the common course of nature, by virtue of the same general laws originally impressed—the same machinery turning out now good, now evil things, and oftener still, the two combined. The division of power is only apparently variable, but really so regular that, were we speaking of human potentates, we should declare without hesitation that the share of each must have been fixed by previous consent. Upon that supposition indeed, the result of the combination of antagonist forces might be much the same as on that of a single creator with divided purposes.

But when we come to consider, not what hypothesis

may be conceived, and possibly reconciled with known facts, but what supposition is pointed to by the evidences of natural religion; the case is different. The indications of design point strongly in one direction, the preservation of the creatures in whose structure the indications are found. Along with the preserving agencies there are destroying agencies, which we might be tempted to ascribe to the will of a different Creator: but there are rarely appearances of the recondite contrivance of means of destruction, except when the destruction of one creature is the means of preservation to others. Nor can it be supposed that the preserving agencies are wielded by one Being, the destroying agencies by another. The destroying agencies are a necessary part of the preserving agencies: the chemical compositions by which life is carried on could not take place without a parallel series of decompositions. The great agent of decay in both organic and inorganic substances is oxidation, and it is only by oxidation that life is continued for even the length of a minute. The imperfections in the attainment of the purposes which the appearances indicate, have not the air of having been designed. They are like the unintended results of accidents insufficiently guarded against, or of a little excess or deficiency in the quantity of some of the agencies by which the good purpose is carried on, or else they are consequences of the wearing out of a machinery not made to last for ever: they point either to short-comings in the workmanship as regards its intended purpose, or to external forces not under the control of the workman, but which forces bear no mark of being wielded and aimed by any other and rival Intelligence.

We may conclude, then, that there is no ground in Natural Theology for attributing intelligence or personality to the obstacles which partially thwart what seem the purposes of the Creator. The limitation of his power more probably results either from the qualities of the material—the substances and forces of which the universe is composed not admitting of any arrangements by which his purposes could be more completely fulfilled; or else, the purposes might have been more fully attained, but the Creator did not know how to do it; creative skill, wonderful as it is, was not sufficiently perfect to accomplish his purposes more thoroughly.

We now pass to the moral attributes of the Deity, so far as indicated in the Creation; or (stating the problem in the broadest manner) to the question, what indications Nature gives of the purposes of its author. This question bears a very different aspect to us from what it bears to those teachers of Natural Theology who are incumbered with the necessity of admitting the omnipotence of the Creator. We have not to attempt the impossible problem of reconciling infinite benevolence and justice with infinite power in

the Creator of such a world as this. The attempt to
do so not only involves absolute contradiction in an
intellectual point of view but exhibits to excess the
revolting spectacle of a jesuitical defence of moral
enormities.

On this topic I need not add to the illustrations
given of this portion of the subject in my Essay on
Nature. At the stage which our argument has
reached there is none of this moral perplexity. Grant
that creative power was limited by conditions the
nature and extent of which are wholly unknown to us,
and the goodness and justice of the Creator may be
all that the most pious believe; and all in the work
that conflicts with those moral attributes may be the
fault of the conditions which left to the Creator only
a choice of evils.

It is, however, one question whether any given
conclusion is consistent with known facts, and another
whether there is evidence to prove it: and if we have
no means for judging of the design but from the work
actually produced, it is a somewhat hazardous speculation to suppose that the work designed was of a
different quality from the result realized. Still, though
the ground is unsafe we may, with due caution,
journey a certain distance on it. Some parts of the
order of nature give much more indication of contrivance than others; many, it is not too much to
say, give no sign of it at all. The signs of con-

trivance are most conspicuous in the structure and
processes of vegetable and animal life. But for these,
it is probable that the appearances in nature would
never have seemed to the thinking part of mankind
to afford any proofs of a God. But when a God had
been inferred from the organization of living beings,
other parts of Nature, such as the structure of the
solar system, seemed to afford evidences, more or less
strong, in confirmation of the belief: granting, then,
a design in Nature, we can best hope to be enlightened as to what that design was, by examining it in
the parts of Nature in which its traces are the most
conspicuous.

To what purpose, then, do the expedients in the
construction of animals and vegetables, which excite
the admiration of naturalists, appear to tend? There
is no blinking the fact that they tend principally to
no more exalted object than to make the structure
remain in life and in working order for a certain time:
the individual for a few years, the species or race for
a longer but still a limited period. And the similar
though less conspicuous marks of creation which are
recognized in inorganic Nature, are generally of the
same character. The adaptations, for instance, which
appear in the solar system consist in placing it under
conditions which enable the mutual action of its parts
to maintain instead of destroying its stability, and
even that only for a time, vast indeed if measured

against our short span of animated existence, but which can be perceived even by us to be limited : for even the feeble means which we possess of exploring the past, are believed by those who have examined the subject by the most recent lights, to yield evidence that the solar system was once a vast sphere of nebula or vapour, and is going through a process which in the course of ages will reduce it to a single and not very large mass of solid matter frozen up with more than arctic cold.   If the machinery of the system is adapted to keep itself at work only for a time, still less perfect is the adaptation of it for the abode of living beings since it is only adapted to them during the relatively short portion of its total duration which intervenes between the time when each planet was too hot and the time when it became or will become too cold to admit of life under the only conditions in which we have experience of its possibility.   Or we should perhaps reverse the statement, and say that organization and life are only adapted to the conditions of the solar system during a relatively short portion of the system's existence.

The greater part, therefore, of the design of which there is indication in Nature, however wonderful its mechanism, is no evidence of any moral attributes, because the end to which it is directed, and its adaptation to which end is the evidence of its being directed to an end at all, is not a moral end: it is not the good of any sentient creature, it is but the qualified permanence, for a limited period, of the work itself, whether animate or inanimate. The only inference that can be drawn from most of it, respecting the character of the Creator, is that he does not wish his works to perish as soon as created; he wills them to have a certain duration. From this alone nothing can be justly inferred as to the manner in which he is affected towards his animate or rational creatures.

After deduction of the great number of adaptations which have no apparent object but to keep the machine going, there remain a certain number of provisions for giving pleasure to living beings, and a certain number of provisions for giving them pain. There is no positive certainty that the whole of these ought not to take their place among the contrivances for keeping the creature or its species in existence; for both the pleasures and the pains have a conservative tendency; the pleasures being generally so disposed as to attract to the things which maintain individual or collective existence, the pains so as to deter from such as would destroy it.

When all these things are considered it is evident that a vast deduction must be made from the evidences of a Creator before they can be counted as evidences of a benevolent purpose: so vast indeed that some may doubt whether after such a deduction there remains any balance. Yet endeavouring to look at the question without partiality or prejudice and without allowing wishes to have any influence over judgment, it does appear that granting the existence of design, there is a preponderance of evidence that the Creator desired the pleasure of his creatures. This is indicated by the fact that pleasure of one description or another is afforded by almost everything, the mere play of the faculties, physical and mental, being a never-ending source of pleasure, and even painful things giving pleasure by the satisfaction of curiosity and the agreeable sense of acquiring knowledge; and also that pleasure, when experienced, seems to result from the normal working of the machinery, while pain usually arises from some external interference with it, and resembles in each particular case the result of an accident. Even in cases when pain results, like pleasure, from the machinery itself, the appearances do not indicate that contrivance was brought into play purposely to produce pain : what is indicated is rather a clumsiness in the contrivance employed for some other purpose. The author of the machinery is no doubt accountable for having made it susceptible of pain ; but this may have been a necessary condition of its susceptibility to pleasure ; a supposition which avails nothing on the theory of an Omnipotent Creator but is an extremely probable one in the case of a contriver working under the limitation of inexorable laws and indestructible properties of matter. The susceptibility being conceded as a thing which did enter into design, the pain itself usually seems like a thing undesigned; a casual result of the collision of the organism with some outward force to which it was not intended to be exposed, and which, in many cases, provision is even made to hinder it from being exposed to. There is, therefore, much appearance that pleasure is agreeable to the Creator, while there is very little if any appearance that pain is so: and there is a certain amount of justification for inferring, on grounds of Natural Theology alone, that benevolence is one of the attributes of the Creator. But to jump from this to the inference that his sole or chief purposes are those of benevolence, and that the single end and aim of Creation was the happiness of his creatures, is not only not justified by any evidence but is a conclusion in opposition to such evidence as we have. If the motive of the Deity for creating sentient beings was the happiness of the beings he created, his purpose, in our corner of the universe at least, must be pronounced, taking past ages and all countries and races into account, to have been thus far an ignominious failure; and if God had no purpose but our happiness and that of other living creatures it is not credible that he would have called them into existence with the prospect of being so completely baffled. If man had not the power by the exercise of his own energies for the improvement both of himself and of his outward circumstances, to do for himself and other creatures vastly more than God had in the first instance done, the Being who called him into existence would deserve something very different from thanks at his hands.  Of course it may be said that this very capacity of improving himself and the world was given to him by God, and that the change which he will be thereby enabled ultimately to effect in human existence will be worth purchasing by the sufferings and wasted lives of entire geological periods.  This may be so ; but to suppose that God could not have given him these blessings at a less frightful cost, is to make a very strange supposition concerning the Deity.  It is to suppose that God could not, in the first instance, create anything better than a Bosjesman or an Andaman islander, or something still lower ; and yet was able to endow the Bosjesman or the Andaman islander with the power of raising himself into a Newton or a Fénelon. We certainly do not know the nature of the barriers which limit the divine omnipotence ; but it is a very odd notion of them that they enable the Deity to confer on an almost bestial creature the power of producing by a succession of efforts what God himself had no other means of creating.

Such are the indications of Natural Religion in

respect to the divine benevolence. If we look for any other of the moral attributes which a certain class of philosophers are accustomed to distinguish from benevolence, as for example Justice, we find a total blank. There is no evidence whatever in Nature for divine justice, whatever standard of justice our ethical opinions may lead us to recognize. There is no shadow of justice in the general arrangements of Nature; and what imperfect realization it obtains in any human society (a most imperfect realization as yet) is the work of man himself, struggling upwards against immense natural difficulties, into civilization, and making to himself a second nature, far better and more unselfish than he was created with. But on this point enough has been said in another Essay, already referred to, on Nature.

These, then, are the net results of Natural Theology on the question of the divine attributes. A Being of great but limited power, how or by what limited we cannot even conjecture; of great, and perhaps unlimited intelligence, but perhaps, also, more narrowly limited than his power: who desires, and pays some regard to, the happiness of his creatures, but who seems to have other motives of action which he cares more for, and who can hardly be supposed to have created the universe for that purpose alone. Such is the Deity whom Natural Religion points to; and any idea of God more captivating than this comes only from human wishes, or from the teaching of either real or imaginary Revelation.

We shall next examine whether the light of nature gives any indications concerning the immortality of the soul, and a future life.

# PART III

## IMMORTALITY

THE indications of immortality may be considered in two divisions: those which are independent of any theory respecting the Creator and his intentions, and those which depend upon an antecedent belief on that subject.

Of the former class of arguments speculative men have in different ages put forward a considerable variety, of which those in the Phædon of Plato are an example; but they are for the most part such as have no adherents, and need not be seriously refuted, now. They are generally founded upon preconceived theories as to the nature of the thinking principle in man, considered as distinct and separable from the body, and on other preconceived theories respecting death. As, for example, that death, or dissolution, is always a separation of parts; and the soul being without parts, being simple and indivisible, is not susceptible of this separation. Curiously enough, one of the interlocutors

in the Phædon anticipates the answer by which an
objector of the present day would meet this argument :
namely, that thought and consciousness, though
mentally distinguishable from the body, may not be a
substance separable from it, but a result of it, standing
in a relation to it (the illustration is Plato's) like that
of a tune to the musical instrument on which it is
played ; and that the arguments used to prove that
the soul does not die with the body, would equally
prove that the tune does not die with the instrument,
but survives its destruction and continues to exist apart.
In fact, those moderns who dispute the evidences of
the immortality of the soul, do not, in general, believe
the soul to be a substance *per se*, but regard it as the
name of a bundle of attributes, the attributes of feeling, thinking, reasoning, believing, willing, &c., and
these attributes they regard as a consequence of the
bodily organization, which therefore, they argue, it is
as unreasonable to suppose surviving when that
organization is dispersed, as to suppose the colour
or odour of a rose surviving when the rose itself has
perished. Those, therefore, who would deduce the
immortality of the soul from its own nature have first
to prove that the attributes in question are not attributes of the body but of a separate substance. Now
what is the verdict of science on this point ? It is not
perfectly conclusive either way. In the first place, it
does not prove, experimentally, that any mode of

organization has the power of producing feeling or thought. To make that proof good it would be necessary that we should be able to produce an organism, and try whether it would feel; which we cannot do; organisms cannot by any human means be produced, they can only be developed out of a previous organism. On the other hand, the evidence is well nigh complete that all thought and feeling has some action of the bodily organism for its immediate antecedent or accompaniment; that the specific variations and especially the different degrees of complication of the nervous and cerebral organization, correspond to differences in the development of the mental faculties; and though we have no evidence, except negative, that the mental consciousness ceases for ever when the functions of the brain are at an end, we do know that diseases of the brain disturb the mental functions and that decay or weakness of the brain enfeebles them. We have therefore sufficient evidence that cerebral action is, if not the cause, at least, in our present state of existence, a condition *sine quá non* of mental operations; and that assuming the mind to be a distinct substance, its separation from the body would not be, as some have vainly flattered themselves, a liberation from trammels and restoration to freedom, but would simply put a stop to its functions and remand it to unconsciousness, unless and until some other set of conditions supervenes, capable of recalling it into activity, but of the existence of which experience does not give us the smallest indication.

At the same time it is of importance to remark that these considerations only amount to defect of evidence; they afford no positive argument against immortality. We must beware of giving *à priori* validity to the conclusions of an *à posteriori* philosophy. The root of all *à priori* thinking is the tendency to transfer to outward things a strong association between the corresponding ideas in our own minds; and the thinkers who most sincerely attempt to limit their beliefs by experience, and honestly believe that they do so, are not always sufficiently on their guard against this mistake. There are thinkers who regard it as a truth of reason that miracles are impossible; and in like manner there are others who because the phenomena of life and consciousness are associated in their minds by undeviating experience with the action of material organs, think it an absurdity *per se* to imagine it possible that those phenomena can exist under any other conditions. But they should remember that the uniform co-existence of one fact with another does not make the one fact a part of the other, or the same with it. The relation of thought to a material brain is no metaphysical necessity; but simply a constant co-existence within the limits of observation. And when analysed to the bottom on the principles of the

Associative Psychology, the brain, just as much as
the mental functions is, like matter itself, merely a
set of human sensations either actual or inferred as
possible, namely those which the anatomist has
when he opens the skull, and the impressions which
we suppose we should receive of molecular or some
other movements when the cerebral action was going
on, if there were no bony envelope and our senses
or our instruments were sufficiently delicate. Experience furnishes us with no example of any series
of states of consciousness, without this group of contingent sensations attached to it ; but it is as easy to
imagine such a series of states without, as with, this
accompaniment, and we know of no reason in the
nature of things against the possibility of its being
thus disjoined. We may suppose that the same
thoughts, emotions, volitions and even sensations
which we have here, may persist or recommence
somewhere else under other conditions, just as we
may suppose that other thoughts and sensations may
exist under other conditions in other parts of the
universe. And in entertaining this supposition we
need not be embarrassed by any metaphysical difficulties about a thinking substance. Substance is but a
general name for the perdurability of attributes :
wherever there is a series of thoughts connected
together by memories, that constitutes a thinking
substance. This absolute distinction in thought and

separability in representation of our states of consciousness from the set of conditions with which they are united only by constancy of concomitance, is equivalent in a practical point of view to the old distinction of the two substances, Matter and Mind.

There is, therefore, in science, no evidence against the immortality of the soul but that negative evidence, which consists in the absence of evidence in its favour. And even the negative evidence is not so strong as negative evidence often is. In the case of witchcraft, for instance, the fact that there is no proof which will stand examination of its having ever existed, is as conclusive as the most positive evidence of its non-existence would be; for it exists, if it does exist, on this earth, where if it had existed the evidence of fact would certainly have been available to prove it. But it is not so as to the soul's existence after death. That it does not remain on earth and go about visibly or interfere in the events of life, is proved by the same weight of evidence which disproves witchcraft. But that it does not exist elsewhere, there is absolutely no proof. A very faint, if any, presumption, is all that is afforded by its disappearance from the surface of this planet.

Some may think that there is an additional and very strong presumption against the immortality of the thinking and conscious principle, from the analysis of all the other objects of Nature. All things in

Nature perish, the most beautiful and perfect being, as philosophers and poets alike complain, the most perishable. A flower of the most exquisite form and colouring grows up from a root, comes to perfection in weeks or months, and lasts only a few hours or days. Why should it be otherwise with man ? Why indeed. But why, also, should it *not* be otherwise ? Feeling and thought are not merely different from what we call inanimate matter, but are at the opposite pole of existence, and analogical inference has little or no validity from the one to the other. Feeling and thought are much more real than anything else; they are the only things which we directly know to be real, all things else being merely the unknown conditions on which these, in our present state of existence or in some other, depend. All matter apart from the feelings of sentient beings has but an hypothetical and unsubstantial existence : it is a mere assumption to account for our sensations; itself we do not perceive, we are not conscious of it, but only of the sensations which we are said to receive from it : in reality it is a mere name for our expectation of sensations, or for our belief that we can have certain sensations when certain other sensations give indication of them. Because these contingent possibilities of sensation sooner or later come to an end and give place to others, is it implied in this, that the series of our feelings must itself be broken

off? This would not be to reason from one kind of
substantive reality to another, but to draw from
something which has no reality except in reference
to something else, conclusions applicable to that
which is the only substantive reality. Mind, (or
whatever name we give to what is implied in consciousness of a continued series of feelings) is in a
philosophical point of view the only reality of which
we have any evidence; and no analogy can be recognized or comparison made between it and other
realities because there are no other known realities
to compare it with. That is quite consistent with
its being perishable; but the question whether it is
so or not is *res integra*, untouched by any of the
results of human knowledge and experience. The
case is one of those very rare cases in which there is
really a total absence of evidence on either side, and
in which the absence of evidence for the affirmative
does not, as in so many cases it does, create a strong
presumption in favour of the negative.

The belief, however, in human immortality, in the
minds of mankind generally, is probably not grounded
on any scientific arguments either physical or metaphysical, but on foundations with most minds much
stronger, namely on one hand the disagreeableness of
giving up existence, (to those at least to whom it has
hitherto been pleasant) and on the other the general
traditions of mankind. The natural tendency of

belief to follow these two inducements, our own wishes and the general assent of other people, has been in this instance reinforced by the utmost exertion of the power of public and private teaching; rulers and instructors having at all times, with the view of giving greater effect to their mandates whether from selfish or from public motives, encouraged to the utmost of their power the belief that there is a life after death, in which pleasures and sufferings far greater than on earth, depend on our doing or leaving undone while alive, what we are commanded to do in the name of the unseen powers. As causes of belief these various circumstances are most powerful. As rational grounds of it they carry no weight at all.

That what is called the consoling nature of an opinion, that is, the pleasure we should have in believing it to be true, can be a ground for believing it, is a doctrine irrational in itself and which would sanction half the mischievous illusions recorded in history or which mislead individual life. It is sometimes, in the case now under consideration, wrapt up in a quasi-scientific language. We are told that the desire of immortality is one of our instincts, and that there is no instinct which has not corresponding to it a real object fitted to satisfy it. Where there is hunger there is somewhere food, where there is sexual feeling there is somewhere sex, where there is love there is somewhere something to be loved, and

so forth : in like manner since there is the instinctive
desire of eternal life, eternal life there must be.   The
answer to this is patent on the very surface of the
subject.   It is unnecessary to go into any recondite
considerations concerning instincts, or to discuss
whether the desire in question is an instinct or not.
Granting that wherever there is an instinct there
exists something such as that instinct demands, can it
be affirmed that this something exists in boundless
quantity, or sufficient to satisfy the infinite craving
of human desires?   What is called the desire of
eternal life is simply the desire of life; and does
there not exist that which this desire calls for?   Is
there not life?   And is not the instinct, if it be an
instinct, gratified by the possession and preservation
of life?   To suppose that the desire of life guarantees
to us personally the reality of life through all
eternity, is like supposing that the desire of food
assures us that we shall always have as much as we
can eat through our whole lives and as much longer
as we can conceive our lives to be protracted to.

The argument from tradition or the general belief
of the human race, if we accept it as a guide to our
own belief, must be accepted entire : if so we are
bound to believe that the souls of human beings not
only survive after death but show themselves as
ghosts to the living; for we find no people who
have had the one belief without the other.   Indeed

it is probable that the former belief originated in the latter, and that primitive men would never have supposed that the soul did not die with the body if they had not fancied that it visited them after death. Nothing could be more natural than such a fancy; it is, in appearance, completely realized in dreams, which in Homer and in all ages like Homer's, are supposed to be real apparitions. To dreams we have to add not merely waking hallucinations but the delusions, however baseless, of sight and hearing, or rather the misinterpretations of those senses, sight or hearing supplying mere hints from which imagination paints a complete picture and invests it with reality. These delusions are not to be judged of by a modern standard: in early times the line between imagination and perception was by no means clearly defined; there was little or none of the knowledge we now possess of the actual course of nature, which makes us distrust or disbelieve any appearance which is at variance with known laws. In the ignorance of men as to what were the limits of nature and what was or was not compatible with it, no one thing seemed, as far as physical considerations went, to be much more improbable than another. In rejecting, therefore, as we do, and as we have the best reason to do, the tales and legends of the actual appearance of disembodied spirits, we take from under the general belief of mankind in a life after death, what in all

probability was its chief ground and support, and
deprive it of even the very little value which the
opinion of rude ages can ever have as evidence of
truth.  If it be said that this belief has maintained
itself in ages which have ceased to be rude and which
reject the superstitions with which it once was accompanied, the same may be said of many other
opinions of rude ages, and especially on the most
important and interesting subjects, because it is on
those subjects that the reigning opinion, whatever it
may be, is the most sedulously inculcated upon all
who are born into the world.  This particular opinion,
moreover, if it has on the whole kept its ground, has
done so with a constantly increasing number of dissentients, and those especially among cultivated
minds.  Finally, those cultivated minds which ad-
here to the belief ground it, we may reasonably suppose, not on the belief of others, but on arguments
and evidences; and those arguments and evidences,
therefore, are what it concerns us to estimate and
judge.

The preceding are a sufficient sample of the arguments for a future life which do not suppose an
antecedent belief in the existence, or any theory
respecting the attributes of the Godhead.  It remains
to consider what arguments are supplied by such
lights, or such grounds of conjecture, as natural
theology affords, on those great questions.

We have seen that these lights are but faint;
that of the existence of a Creator they afford no
more than a preponderance of probability; of his
benevolence a considerably less preponderance; that
there is, however, some reason to think that he cares
for the pleasures of his creatures, but by no means
that this is his sole care, or that other purposes do
not often take precedence of it. His intelligence
must be adequate to the contrivances apparent in
the universe, but need not be more than adequate
to them, and his power is not only not proved
to be infinite, but the only real evidences in natural
theology tend to show that it is limited, contrivance
being a mode of overcoming difficulties, and always
supposing difficulties to be overcome.

We have now to consider what inference can
legitimately be drawn from these premises, in favour
of a future life. It seems to me, apart from express
revelation, none at all.

The common arguments are, the goodness of God;
the improbability that he would ordain the annihilation of his noblest and richest work, after the greater
part of its few years of life had been spent in the
acquisition of faculties which time is not allowed
him to turn to fruit; and the special improbability
that he would have implanted in us an instinctive
desire of eternal life, and doomed that desire to
complete disappointment.

These might be arguments in a world the constitution of which made it possible without contradiction to hold it for the work of a Being at once omnipotent and benevolent. But they are not arguments in a world like that in which we live. The benevolence of the divine Being may be perfect, but his power being subject to unknown limitations, we know not that he could have given us what we so confidently assert that he must have given; *could* (that is) without sacrificing something more important. Even his benevolence, however justly inferred, is by no means indicated as the interpretation of his whole purpose, and since we cannot tell how far other purposes may have interfered with the exercise of his benevolence, we know not that he *would*, even if he could have granted us eternal life. With regard to the supposed improbability of his having given the wish without its gratification, the same answer may be made; the scheme which either limitation of power, or conflict of purposes, compelled him to adopt, may have *required* that we should have the wish although it were not destined to be gratified. One thing, however, is quite certain in respect to God's government of the world; that he either could not, or would not, grant to us every thing we wish. We wish for life, and he has granted some life: that we wish (or some of us wish) for a boundless extent of life and that it is not granted, is no exception to the ordinary modes of his government. Many a man would like to be a Crœsus or an Augustus Cæsar, but has his wishes gratified only to the moderate extent of a pound a week or the Secretaryship of his Trades Union. There is, therefore, no assurance whatever of a life after death, on grounds of natural religion. But to any one who feels it conducive either to his satisfaction or to his usefulness to hope for a future state as a possibility, there is no hindrance to his indulging that hope. Appearances point to the existence of a Being who has great power over us—all the power implied in the creation of the Kosmos, or of its organized beings at least—and of whose goodness we have evidence though not of its being his predominant attribute: and as we do not know the limits either of his power or of his goodness, there is room to hope that both the one and the other may extend to granting us this gift provided that it would really be beneficial to us. The same ground which permits the hope warrants us in expecting that if there be a future life it will be at least as good as the present, and will not be wanting in the best feature of the present life, improvability by our own efforts. Nothing can be more opposed to every estimate we can form of probability, than the common idea of the future life as a state of rewards and punishments in any other sense than that the consequences of our actions upon our own character and susceptibilities will follow us in the future as they have done in the past and present. Whatever be the probabilities *of* a future life, all the probabilities *in case of* a future life are that such as we have been made or have made ourselves before the change, such we shall enter into the life hereafter; and that the fact of death will make no sudden break in our spiritual life, nor influence our character any otherwise than as any important change in our mode of existence may always be expected to modify it. Our thinking principle has its laws which in this life are invariable, and any analogies drawn from this life must assume that the same laws will continue. To imagine that a miracle will be wrought at death by the act of God making perfect every one whom it is his will to include among his elect, might be justified by an express revelation duly authenticated, but is utterly opposed to every presumption that can be deduced from the light of Nature.

# PART IV

## REVELATION

THE discussion in the preceding pages respecting the evidences of Theism has been strictly confined to those which are derived from the light of Nature. It is a different question what addition has been made to those evidences, and to what extent the conclusions obtainable from them have been amplified or modified, by the establishment of a direct communication with the Supreme Being. It would be beyond the purpose of this Essay, to take into consideration the positive evidences of the Christian, or any other belief, which claims to be a revelation from Heaven. But such general considerations as are applicable not to a particular system, but to Revelation generally, may properly find a place here, and are indeed necessary to give a sufficiently practical bearing to the results of the preceding investigation.

In the first place, then, the indications of a Creator and of his attributes which we have been able to find in Nature, though so much slighter and less conclusive even as to his existence than the pious mind would wish to consider them, and still more unsatisfactory in the information they afford as to his attributes, are yet sufficient to give to the supposition of a Revelation a standing point which it would not otherwise have had. The alleged Revelation is not obliged to build up its case from the foundation; it has not to prove the very existence of the Being from whom it professes to come. It claims to be a message from a Being whose existence, whose power, and to a certain extent whose wisdom and goodness, are, if not proved, at least indicated with more or less of probability by the phenomena of Nature. The sender of the alleged message is not a sheer invention; there are grounds independent of the message itself for belief in his reality; grounds which, though insufficient for proof, are sufficient to take away all antecedent improbability from the supposition that a message may really have been received from him. It is, moreover, much to the purpose to take notice, that the very imperfection of the evidences which Natural Theology can produce of the Divine attributes, removes some of the chief stumbling blocks to the belief of a Revelation; since the objections grounded on imperfections in the Revelation itself, however conclusive against it if it is considered as a record of the acts or an expression of the wisdom

of a Being of infinite power combined with infinite
wisdom and goodness, are no reason whatever against
its having come from a Being such as the course of
nature points to, whose wisdom is possibly, his power
certainly, limited, and whose goodness, though real,
is not likely to have been the only motive which
actuated him in the work of Creation. The argument
of Butler's Analogy, is, from its own point of view,
conclusive : the Christian religion is open to no objections, either moral or intellectual, which do not apply
at least equally to the common theory of Deism; the
morality of the Gospels is far higher and better than
that which shows itself in the order of Nature; and
what is morally objectionable in the Christian theory
of the world, is objectionable only when taken in conjunction with the doctrine of an omnipotent God :
and (at least as understood by the most enlightened
Christians) by no means imports any moral obliquity
in a Being whose power is supposed to be restricted
by real, though unknown obstacles, which prevented
him from fully carrying out his design. The grave
error of Butler was that he shrank from admitting
the hypothesis of limited powers; and his appeal consequently amounts to this : The belief of Christians is neither more absurd nor more immoral than
the belief of Deists who acknowledge an Omnipotent
Creator, let us, therefore, in spite of the absurdity and
immorality, believe both. He ought to have said, let

us cut down our belief of either to what does not involve absurdity or immorality; to what is neither intellectually self-contradictory nor morally perverted.

To return, however, to the main subject : on the hypothesis of a God, who made the world, and in making it had regard, however that regard may have been limited by other considerations, to the happiness of his sentient creatures, there is no antecedent improbability in the supposition that his concern for their good would continue, and that he might once or oftener give proof of it by communicating to them some knowledge of himself beyond what they were able to make out by their unassisted faculties, and some knowledge or precepts useful for guiding them through the difficulties of life. Neither on the only tenable hypothesis, that of limited power, is it open to us to object that these helps ought to have been greater, or in any way other than they are. The only question to be entertained, and which we cannot dispense ourselves from entertaining, is that of evidence. Can any evidence suffice to prove a Divine Revelation ? And of what nature, and what amount, must that evidence be ? Whether the special evidences of Christianity, or of any other alleged revelation, do or do not come up to the mark, is a different question, into which I do not propose directly to enter. The question I intend to consider, is, what evidence is required ; what general conditions it ought to satisfy ;

and whether they are such as, according to the known constitution of things, *can* be satisfied.

The evidences of Revelation are commonly distinguished as external or internal. External evidences are the testimony of the senses or of witnesses. By the internal evidences are meant the indications which the Revelation itself is thought to furnish of its divine origin; indications supposed to consist chiefly in the excellence of its precepts, and its general suitability to the circumstances and needs of human nature.

The consideration of these internal evidences is very important, but their importance is principally negative; they may be conclusive grounds for rejecting a Revelation, but cannot of themselves warrant the acceptance of it as divine. If the moral character of the doctrines of an alleged Revelation is bad and perverting, we ought to reject it from whomsoever it comes; for it cannot come from a good and wise Being. But the excellence of their morality can never entitle us to ascribe to them a supernatural origin: for we cannot have conclusive reason for believing that the human faculties were incompetent to find out moral doctrines of which the human faculties can perceive and recognize the excellence. A Revelation, therefore, cannot be proved divine unless by external evidence; that is, by the exhibition of supernatural facts. And we have to consider, whether it is possible to prove supernatural facts, and if it is, what evidence is required to prove them.

This question has only, so far as I know, been seriously raised on the sceptical side, by Hume. It is the question involved in his famous argument against Miracles: an argument which goes down to the depths of the subject, but the exact scope and effect of which, (perhaps not conceived with perfect correctness by that great thinker himself), have in general been utterly misconceived by those who have attempted to answer him. Dr. Campbell, for example, one of the acutest of his antagonists, has thought himself obliged, in order to support the credibility of miracles, to lay down doctrines which virtually go the length of maintaining that antecedent improbability is never a sufficient ground for refusing credence to a statement, if it is well attested. Dr. Campbell's fallacy lay in overlooking a double meaning of the word improbability; as I have pointed out in my Logic, and, still earlier, in an editorial note to Bentham's treatise on Evidence.

Taking the question from the very beginning; it is evidently impossible to maintain that if a supernatural fact really occurs, proof of its occurrence cannot be accessible to the human faculties. The evidence of our senses could prove this as it can prove other things. To put the most extreme case: suppose that I actually saw and heard a Being, either

of the human form, or of some form previously unknown to me, commanding a world to exist, and a
new world actually starting into existence and commencing a movement through space, at his command.
There can be no doubt that this evidence would
convert the creation of worlds from a speculation
into a fact of experience. It may be said, I could
not know that so singular an appearance was anything more than a hallucination of my senses. True;
but the same doubt exists at first respecting every
unsuspected and surprising fact which comes to light
in our physical researches. That our senses have
been deceived, is a possibility which has to be met
and dealt with, and we do deal with it by several
means. If we repeat the experiment, and again with
the same result; if at the time of the observation the
impressions of our senses are in all other respects the
same as usual, rendering the supposition of their
being morbidly affected in this one particular, extremely improbable; above all, if other people's
senses confirm the testimony of our own; we conclude, with reason, that we may trust our senses.
Indeed our senses are all that we have to trust to.
We depend on them for the ultimate premises even
of our reasonings. There is no other appeal against
their decision than an appeal from the senses without
precautions to the senses with all due precautions.
When the evidence, on which an opinion rests, is

equal to that upon which the whole conduct and safety of our lives is founded, we need ask no further. Objections which apply equally to all evidence are valid against none. They only prove abstract fallibility.

But the evidence of miracles, at least to Protestant Christians, is not, in our own day, of this cogent description. It is not the evidence of our senses, but of witnesses, and even this not at first hand, but resting on the attestation of books and traditions. And even in the case of the original eye-witnesses, the supernatural facts asserted on their alleged testimony, are not of the transcendant character supposed in our example, about the nature of which, or the impossibility of their having had a natural origin, there could be little room for doubt. On the contrary, the recorded miracles are, in the first place, generally such as it would have been extremely difficult to verify as matters of fact, and in the next place, are hardly ever beyond the possibility of having been brought about by human means or by the spontaneous agencies of nature. It is to cases of this kind that Hume's argument against the credibility of miracles was meant to apply.

His argument is : The evidence of miracles consists of testimony. The ground of our reliance on testimony is our experience that certain conditions being supposed, testimony is generally veracious. But the same experience tells us that even under the best conditions testimony is frequently either intentionally or un-intentionally, false. When, therefore, the fact to which testimony is produced is one the happening of which would be more at variance with experience than the falsehood of testimony, we ought not to believe it. And this rule all prudent persons observe in the conduct of life. Those who do not, are sure to suffer for their credulity.

Now a miracle (the argument goes on to say) is, in the highest possible degree, contradictory to experience: for if it were not contradictory to experience it would not be a miracle. The very reason for its being regarded as a miracle is that it is a breach of a law of nature, that is, of an otherwise invariable and inviolable uniformity in the succession of natural events. There is, therefore, the very strongest reason for disbelieving it, that experience can give for disbelieving anything. But the mendacity or error of witnesses, even though numerous and of fair character, is quite within the bounds of even common experience. That supposition, therefore, ought to be preferred.

There are two apparently weak points in this argument. One is, that the evidence of experience to which its appeal is made is only negative evidence, which is not so conclusive as positive; since facts of which there had been no previous experience are often

discovered, and proved by positive experience to
be true. The other seemingly vulnerable point is
this. The argument has the appearance of assuming
that the testimony of experience against miracles is
undeviating and indubitable, as it would be if the
whole question was about the probability of future
miracles, none having taken place in the past ; whereas
the very thing asserted on the other side is that
there have been miracles, and that the testimony of
experience is not wholly on the negative side. All
the evidence alleged in favour of any miracle ought to
be reckoned as counter evidence in refutation of the
ground on which it is asserted that miracles ought to
be disbelieved. The question can only be stated fairly
as depending on a balance of evidence : a certain
amount of positive evidence in favour of miracles, and
a negative presumption from the general course of
human experience against them.

In order to support the argument under this double
correction, it has to be shown that the negative presumption against a miracle is very much stronger than
that against a merely new and surprising fact. This,
however, is evidently the case. A new physical
discovery even if it consists in the defeating of a well
established law of nature, is but the discovery of
another law previously unknown. There is nothing
in this but what is familiar to our experience : we were
aware that we did not know all the laws of nature,

and we were aware that one such law is liable to be
counteracted by others. The new phenomenon, when
brought to light, is found still to depend on law; it is
always exactly reproduced when the same circumstances are repeated. Its occurrence, therefore, is
within the limits of variation in experience, which
experience itself discloses. But a miracle, in the very
fact of being a miracle, declares itself to be a supersession not of one natural law by another, but of the
law which includes all others, which experience shows
to be universal for all phenomena, viz., that they
depend on some law; that they are always the same
when there are the same phenomenal antecedents, and
neither take place in the absence of their phenomenal
causes, nor ever fail to take place when the phenomenal
conditions are all present.

It is evident that this argument against belief in
miracles had very little to rest upon until a com-
paratively modern stage in the progress of science. A
few generations ago the universal dependence of
phenomena on invariable laws was not only not recognized by mankind in general but could not be
regarded by the instructed as a scientifically established
truth. There were many phenomena which seemed
quite irregular in their course, without dependence on
any known antecedents: and though, no doubt, a
certain regularity in the occurrence of the most familiar phenomena must always have been recognized,

yet, even in these, the exceptions which were constantly occurring had not yet, by an investigation and generalization of the circumstances of their occurrence, been reconciled with the general rule. The heavenly bodies were from of old the most conspicuous types of regular and unvarying order : yet even among them comets were a phenomenon apparently originating without any law, and eclipses, one which seemed to take place in violation of law. Accordingly both comets and eclipses long continued to be regarded as of a miraculous nature, intended as signs and omens of human fortunes. It would have been impossible in those days to prove to any one that this supposition was antecedently improbable. It seemed more conformable to appearances than the hypothesis of an unknown law.

Now, however, when, in the progress of science, all phenomena have been shown, by indisputable evidence, to be amenable to law, and even in the cases in which those laws have not yet been exactly ascertained, delay in ascertaining them is fully accounted for by the special difficulties of the subject; the defenders of miracles have adapted their argument to this altered state of things, by maintaining that a miracle need not necessarily be a violation of law. It may, they say, take place in fulfilment of a more recondite law, to us unknown.

If by this it be only meant that the Divine Being, in the exercise of his power of interfering with and suspending his own laws, guides himself by some general principle or rule of action, this, of course, cannot be disproved, and is in itself the most probable supposition. But if the argument means that a miracle may be the fulfilment of a law in the same sense in which the ordinary events of Nature are fulfilments of laws, it seems to indicate an imperfect conception of what is meant by a law, and of what constitutes a miracle.

When we say that an ordinary physical fact always takes place according to some invariable law, we mean that it is connected by uniform sequence or coexistence with some definite set of physical antecedents; that whenever that set is exactly reproduced the same phenomenon will take place, unless counteracted by the similar laws of some other physical antecedents; and that whenever it does take place, it would always be found that its special set of antecedents (or one of its sets if it has more than one) has pre-existed. Now, an event which takes place in this manner, is not a miracle. To make it a miracle it must be produced by a direct volition, without the use of means; or at least, of any means which if simply repeated would produce it. To constitute a miracle a phenomenon must take place without having been preceded by any antecedent phenomenal conditions sufficient again to reproduce it; or a phenomenon for the production of which the antecedent conditions existed,

must be arrested or prevented without the intervention of any phenomenal antecedents which would
arrest or prevent it in a future case. The test of a
miracle is: Were there present in the case such external conditions, such second causes we may call
them, that whenever these conditions or causes re-
appear the event will be reproduced? If there were,
it is not a miracle; if there were not, it is a miracle,
but it is not according to law: it is an event produced,
without, or in spite of law.

It will perhaps be said that a miracle does not
necessarily exclude the intervention of second causes.
If it were the will of God to raise a thunderstorm by
miracle, he might do it by means of winds and clouds.
Undoubtedly; but the winds and clouds were either
sufficient when produced to excite the thunderstorm
without other divine assistance, or they were not. If
they were not, the storm is not a fulfilment of law,
but a violation of it. If they were sufficient, there is
a miracle, but it is not the storm; it is the production
of the winds and clouds, or whatever link in the chain
of causation it was at which the influence of physical
antecedents was dispensed with. If that influence
was never dispensed with, but the event called miraculous was produced by natural means, and those again
by others, and so on from the beginning of things;
if the event is no otherwise the act of God than in
having been foreseen and ordained by him as the

consequence of the forces put in action at the Creation ; then there is no miracle at all, nor anything different from the ordinary working of God's providence.

For another example : a person professing to be divinely commissioned, cures a sick person, by some apparently insignificant external application. Would this application, administered by a person not specially commissioned from above, have effected the cure ? If so, there is no miracle ; if not, there is a miracle, but there is a violation of law.

It will be said, however, that if these be violations of law, then law is violated every time that any outward effect is produced by a voluntary act of a human being. Human volition is constantly modifying natural phenomena, not by violating their laws, but by using their laws. Why may not divine volition do the same ? The power of volitions over phenomena is itself a law, and one of the earliest known and acknowledged laws of nature. It is true, the human will exercises power over objects in general indirectly, through the direct power which it possesses only over the human muscles. God, however, has direct power not merely over one thing, but over all the objects which he has made. There is, therefore, no more a supposition of violation of law in supposing that events are produced, prevented, or modified by God's action, than in the supposition of their being produced, prevented, or modified by man's action.

Both are equally in the course of nature, both equally consistent with what we know of the government of all things by law.

Those who thus argue are mostly believers in Free Will, and maintain that every human volition originates a new chain of causation, of which it is itself the commencing link, not connected by invariable sequence with any anterior fact. Even, therefore, if a divine interposition did constitute a breaking-in upon the connected chain of events, by the introduction of a new originating cause without root in the past, this would be no reason for discrediting it, since every human act of volition does precisely the same. If the one is a breach of law, so are the others. In fact, the reign of law does not extend to the origination of volition.

Those who dispute the Free Will theory, and regard volition as no exception to the Universal law of Cause and Effect, may answer, that volitions do not interrupt the chain of causation, but carry it on, the connection of cause and effect being of just the same nature between motive and act as between a combination of physical antecedents and a physical consequent. But this, whether true or not, does not really affect the argument: for the interference of human will with the course of nature is only not an exception to law when we include among laws the relation of motive to volition; and by the same rule interference by the

Divine will would not be an exception either; since we cannot but suppose the Deity, in every one of his acts, to be determined by motives.

The alleged analogy therefore holds good: but what it proves is only what I have from the first maintained—that divine interference with nature could be proved if we had the same sort of evidence for it which we have for human interferences. The question of antecedent improbability only arises because divine interposition is not certified by the direct evidence of perception, but is always matter of inference, and more or less of speculative inference. And a little consideration will show that in these circumstances the antecedent presumption against the truth of the inference is extremely strong.

When the human will interferes to produce any physical phenomenon, except the movements of the human body, it does so by the employment of means: and is obliged to employ·such means as are by their own physical properties sufficient to bring about the effect. Divine interference, by hypothesis, proceeds in a different manner from this : it produces its effect without means, or with such as are in themselves insufficient. In the first case, all the physical phenomena except the first bodily movement are produced in strict conformity to physical causation; while that first movement is traced by positive observation, to the cause (the volition) which pro-

duced it. In the other case, the event is supposed
not to have been produced at all through physical
causation, while there is no direct evidence to connect it with any volition. The ground on which
it is ascribed to a volition is only negative, because
there is no other apparent way of accounting for its
existence.

But in this merely speculative explanation there
is always another hypothesis possible, viz., that the
event may have been produced by physical causes, in
a manner not apparent. It may either be due to a
law of physical nature not yet known, or to the unknown presence of the conditions necessary for producing it according to some known law. Supposing
even that the event, supposed to be miraculous,
does not reach us through the uncertain medium of
human testimony but rests on the direct evidence of
our own senses ; even then so long as there is no
direct evidence of its production by a divine volition,
like that we have for the production of bodily movements by human volitions—so long, therefore, as the
miraculous character of the event is but an inference
from the supposed inadequacy of the laws of physical
nature to account for it,—so long will the hypothesis
of a natural origin for the phenomenon be entitled to
preference over that of a supernatural one. The
commonest principles of sound judgment forbid us
to suppose for any effect a cause of which we have

absolutely no experience, unless all those of which we have experience are ascertained to be absent. Now there are few things of which we have more frequent experience than of physical facts which our knowledge does not enable us to account for, because they depend either on laws which observation, aided by science, has not yet brought to light, or on facts the presence of which in the particular case is un-suspected by us. Accordingly when we hear of a prodigy we always, in these modern times, believe that if it really occurred it was neither the work of God nor of a demon, but the consequence of some unknown natural law or of some hidden fact. Nor is either of these suppositions precluded when, as in the case of a miracle properly so called, the wonderful event seemed to depend upon the will of a human being. It is always possible that there may be at work some undetected law of nature which the wonder-worker may have acquired, consciously or un-consciously, the power of calling into action ; or that the wonder may have been wrought (as in the truly extraordinary feats of jugglers) by the employment, unperceived by us, of ordinary laws : which also need not necessarily be a case of voluntary deception ; or, lastly, the event may have had no connection with the volition at all, but the coincidence between them may be the effect of craft or accident, the miracle-worker having seemed or affected to produce by his

will that which was already about to take place, as
if one were to command an eclipse of the sun at the
moment when one knew by astronomy that an eclipse
was on the point of taking place. In a case of this
description, the miracle might be tested by a
challenge to repeat it; but it is worthy of remark,
that recorded miracles were seldom or never put to
this test. No miracle-worker seems ever to have
made a *practice* of raising the dead: that and the
other most signal of the miraculous operations are
reported to have been performed only in one or a few
isolated cases, which may have been either cunningly
selected cases, or accidental coincidences. There is,
in short, nothing to exclude the supposition that
every alleged miracle was due to natural causes: and
as long as that supposition remains possible, no
scientific observer, and no man of ordinary practical
judgment, would assume by conjecture a cause which
no reason existed for supposing to be real, save
the necessity of accounting for something which is
sufficiently accounted for without it.

Were we to stop here, the case against miracles
might seem to be complete. But on further inspec-
tion it will be seen that we cannot, from the above
considerations, conclude absolutely that the miraculous theory of the production of a phenomenon ought
to be at once rejected. We can conclude only that
no extraordinary powers which have ever been alleged

to be exercised by any human being over nature, can be evidence of miraculous gifts to any one to whom the existence of a supernatural Being, and his interference in human affairs, is not already a *vera causa.* The existence of God cannot possibly be proved by miracles, for unless a God is already recognized, the apparent miracle can always be accounted for on a more probable hypothesis than that of the interference of a Being of whose very existence it is supposed to be the sole evidence. Thus far Hume's argument is conclusive. But it is far from being equally so when the existence of a Being who created the present order of Nature, and, therefore, may well be thought to have power to modify it, is accepted as a fact, or even as a probability resting on independent evidence. Once admit a God, and the production by his direct volition of an effect which in any case owed its origin to his creative will, is no longer a purely arbitrary hypothesis to account for the fact, but must be reckoned with as a serious possibility. The question then changes its character, and the decision of it must now rest upon what is known or reasonably surmised as to the manner of God's government of the universe : whether this knowledge or surmise makes it the more probable supposition that the event was brought about by the agencies by which his government is ordinarily carried on, or that it is the result of a special and

extraordinary interposition of his will in supersession
of those ordinary agencies.

In the first place, then, assuming as a fact the
existence and providence of God, the whole of our
observation of Nature proves to us by incontrover-
tible evidence that the rule of his government is by
means of second causes; that all facts, or at least all
physical facts, follow uniformly upon given physical
conditions, and never occur but when the appropriate
collection of physical conditions is realized. I limit
the assertion to physical facts, in order to leave the
case of human volition an open question: though
indeed I need not do so, for if the human will is
free, it has been left free by the Creator, and is not
controlled by him either through second causes or
directly, so that, not being governed, it is not a spe-
cimen of his mode of government. Whatever he
does govern, he governs by second causes. This was
not obvious in the infancy of science; it was more
and more recognized as the processes of nature were
more carefully and accurately examined, until there
now remains no class of phenomena of which it is
not positively known, save some cases which from
their obscurity and complication our scientific processes have not yet been able completely to clear up
and disentangle, and in which, therefore, the proof
that they also are governed by natural laws could
not, in the present state of science, be more complete.

The evidence, though merely negative, which these circumstances afford that government by second causes is universal, is admitted for all except directly religious purposes to be conclusive. When either a man of science for scientific or a man of the world for practical purposes inquires into an event, he asks himself what is its cause? and not, has it any natural cause? A man would be laughed at who set down as one of the alternative suppositions that there is no other cause for it than the will of God.

Against this weight of negative evidence we have to set such positive evidence as is produced in attestation of exceptions; in other words, the positive evidences of miracles. And I have already admitted that this evidence might conceivably have been such as to make the exception equally certain with the rule. If we had the direct testimony of our senses to a supernatural fact, it might be as completely authenticated and made certain as any natural one. But we never have. The supernatural character of the fact is always, as I have said, matter of inference and speculation: and the mystery always admits the possibility of a solution not supernatural. To those who already believe in supernatural power, the supernatural hypothesis may appear more probable than the natural one; but only if it accords with what we know or reasonably surmise respecting the ways of the supernatural agent. Now all that we know, from the evidence of nature, concerning his ways, is in harmony with the natural theory and repugnant to the supernatural. There is, therefore, a vast preponderance of probability against a miracle, to counterbalance which would require a very extraordinary and indisputable congruity in the supposed miracle and its circumstances with something which we conceive ourselves to know, or to have grounds for believing, with regard to the divine attributes.

This extraordinary congruity is supposed to exist when the purpose of the miracle is extremely beneficial to mankind, as when it serves to accredit some highly important belief. The goodness of God, it is supposed, affords a high degree of antecedent probability that he would make an exception to his general rule of government, for so excellent a purpose. For reasons, however, which have already been entered into, any inference drawn by us from the goodness of God to what he has or has not actually done, is to the last degree precarious. If we reason directly from God's goodness to positive facts, no misery, nor vice nor crime ought to exist in the world. We can see no reason in God's goodness why if he deviated once from the ordinary system of his government in order to do good to man, he should not have done so on a hundred other occasions; nor why, if the benefit aimed at by some given deviation, such as the revelation of Christianity, was transcendent and unique, that precious gift should only have been vouchsafed after the lapse of many ages; or why, when it was at last given, the evidence of it should have been left open to so much doubt and difficulty. Let it be remembered also that the goodness of God affords no presumption in favour of a deviation from his general system of government unless the good purpose could not have been attained without deviation. If God intended that mankind should receive Christianity or any other gift, it would have agreed better with all that we know of his government to have made provision in the scheme of creation for its arising at the appointed time by natural development; which, let it be added, all the knowledge we now possess concerning the history of the human mind, tends to the conclusion that it actually did.

To all these considerations ought to be added the extremely imperfect nature of the testimony itself which we possess for the miracles, real or supposed, which accompanied the foundation of Christianity and of every other revealed religion. Take it at the best, it is the uncross-examined testimony of extremely ignorant people, credulous as such usually are, honourably credulous when the excellence of the doctrine or just reverence for the teacher makes them eager to believe; unaccustomed to draw the line between the perceptions of sense, and what is superinduced upon them by the suggestions of a lively imagination; un-

versed in the difficult art of deciding between appearance and reality, and between the natural and the
supernatural; in times, moreover, when no one thought
it worth while to contradict any alleged miracle,
because it was the belief of the age that miracles in
themselves proved nothing, since they could be worked
by a lying spirit as well as by the spirit of God.
Such were the witnesses; and even of them we do not
possess the direct testimony; the documents, of date long
subsequent, even on the orthodox theory, which contain
the only history of these events, very often do not
even name the supposed eye-witnesses. They put
down (it is but just to admit), the best and least absurd
of the wonderful stories such multitudes of which were
current among the early Christians; but when they
do, exceptionally, name any of the persons who were
the subjects or spectators of the miracle, they doubtless
draw from tradition, and mention those names with
which the story was in the popular mind, (perhaps
accidentally) connected : for whoever has observed the
way in which even now a story grows up from some
small foundation, taking on additional details at every
step, knows well how from being at first anonymous
it gets names attached to it; the name of some one
by whom perhaps the story has been told, being brought
into the story itself first as a witness, and still later
as a party concerned.

It is also noticeable and is a very important consideration, that stories of miracles only grow up among the ignorant and are adopted, if ever, by the educated when they have already become the belief of multitudes. Those which are believed by Protestants all originate in ages and nations in which there was hardly any canon of probability, and miracles were thought to be among the commonest of all phenomena. The Catholic Church, indeed, holds as an article of faith that miracles have never ceased, and new ones continue to be now and then brought forth and believed, even in the present incredulous age—yet if in an incredulous generation certainly not among the incredulous portion of it, but always among people who, in addition to the most childish ignorance, have grown up (as all do who are educated by the Catholic clergy) trained in the persuasion that it is a duty to believe and a sin to doubt ; that it is dangerous to be sceptical about anything which is tendered for belief in the name of the true religion ; and that nothing is so contrary to piety as incredulity. But these miracles which no one but a Roman Catholic, and by no means every Roman Catholic believes, rest frequently upon an amount of testimony greatly surpassing that which we possess for any of the early miracles ; and superior especially in one of the most essential points, that in many cases the alleged eye-witnesses are known, and we have their story at first hand.

Thus, then, stands the balance of evidence in respect to the reality of miracles, assuming the existence and government of God to be proved by other evidence. On the one side, the great negative presumption arising from the whole of what the course of nature discloses to us of the divine government, as carried on through second causes and by invariable sequences of physical effects upon constant antecedents. On the other side, a few exceptional instances, attested by evidence not of a character to warrant belief in any facts in the smallest degree unusual or improbable; the eye-witnesses in most cases unknown, in none competent by character or education to scrutinize the real nature of the appearances which they may have seen,* and moved moreover by a union of the strongest motives which can inspire human beings to persuade, first themselves, and then others, that what they had seen was a miracle. The facts, too, even if faithfully reported, are never incompatible with the supposition that they were either mere coincidences, or were produced by natural means; even when no specific conjecture can be made as to those means, which in general it can. The conclusion I draw is that miracles have no claim whatever to the character of historical facts and are wholly invalid as evidences of any revelation.

What can be said with truth on the side of miracles

---

* St. Paul, the only known exception to the ignorance and want of education of the first generation of Christians, attests no miracle but that of his own conversion, which of all the miracles of the New Testament is the one which admits of the easiest explanation from natural causes.

amounts only to this: Considering that the order of
nature affords some evidence of the reality of a
Creator, and of his bearing good will to his creatures
though not of its being the sole prompter of his conduct towards them : considering, again, that all the
evidence of his existence is evidence also that he is
not all-powerful, and considering that in our ignorance of the limits of his power we cannot positively
decide that he was able to provide for us by the
original plan of Creation all the good which it
entered into his intentions to bestow upon us,
or even to bestow any part of it at any earlier
period than that at which we actually received it
—considering these things, when we consider further
that a gift, extremely precious, came to us which
though facilitated was not apparently necessitated by
what had gone before, but was due, as far as appearances go, to the peculiar mental and moral endowments of one man, and that man openly proclaimed
that it did not come from himself but from God
through him, then we are entitled to say that there is
nothing so inherently impossible or absolutely in-
credible in this supposition as to preclude any one
from hoping that it may perhaps be true. I say
from hoping ; I go no further ; for I cannot attach
any evidentiary value to the testimony even of Christ
on such a subject, since he is never said to have
declared any evidence of his mission (unless his own

interpretations of the Prophecies be so considered) except internal conviction; and everybody knows that in prescientific times men always supposed that any unusual faculties which came to them they knew not how, were an inspiration from God; the best men always being the readiest to ascribe any honourable peculiarity in themselves to that higher source, rather than to their own merits.

# PART V

## GENERAL RESULT

FROM the result of the preceding examination of the evidences of Theism, and (Theism being presupposed) of the evidences of any Revelation, it follows that the rational attitude of a thinking mind towards the supernatural, whether in natural or in revealed religion, is that of scepticism as distinguished from belief on the one hand, and from atheism on the other : including, in the present case, under atheism, the negative as well as the positive form of disbelief in a God, viz., not only the dogmatic denial of his existence, but the denial that there is any evidence on either side, which for most practical purposes amounts to the same thing as if the existence of a God had been disproved. If we are right in the conclusions to which we have been led by the preceding inquiry there is evidence, but insufficient for proof, and amounting only to one of the lower degrees of probability. The indication given by such evidence

as there is, points to the creation, not indeed of the
universe, but of the present order of it by an Intelligent Mind, whose power over the materials was
not absolute, whose love for his creatures was not his
sole actuating inducement, but who nevertheless
desired their good. The notion of a providential
government by an omnipotent Being for the good
of his creatures must be entirely dismissed. Even
of the continued existence of the Creator we have
no other guarantee than that he cannot be subject
to the law of death which affects terrestrial beings,
since the conditions that produce this liability
wherever it is known to exist are of his creating.
That this Being, not being omnipotent, may have
produced a machinery falling short of his intentions,
and which may require the occasional interposition
of the Maker's hand, is a supposition not in itself
absurd nor impossible, though in none of the cases in
which such interposition is believed to have occurred
is the evidence such as could possibly prove it; it
remains a simple possibility, which those may dwell
on to whom it yields comfort to suppose that blessings
which ordinary human power is inadequate to attain,
may come not from extraordinary human power, but
from the bounty of an intelligence beyond the human,
and which continuously cares for man. The possibility of a life after death rests on the same footing—
of a boon which this powerful Being who wishes

well to man, may have the power to grant, and which if the message alleged to have been sent by him was really sent, he has actually promised. The whole domain of the supernatural is thus removed from the region of Belief into that of simple Hope; and in that, for anything we can see, it is likely always to remain ; for we can hardly anticipate either that any positive evidence will be acquired of the direct agency of Divine Benevolence in human destiny, or that any reason will be discovered for considering the realization of human hopes on that subject as beyond the pale of possibility.

It is now to be considered whether the indulgence of hope, in a region of imagination merely, in which there is no prospect that any probable grounds of expectation will ever be obtained, is irrational, and ought to be discouraged as a departure from the rational principle of regulating our feelings as well as opinions strictly by evidence.

This is a point which different thinkers are likely, for a long time at least, to decide differently, according to their individual temperament. The principles which ought to govern the cultivation and the regulation of the imagination—with a view on the one hand of preventing it from disturbing the rectitude of the intellect and the right direction of the actions and will, and on the other hand of employing it as a power for increasing the happiness of life and giving elevation to the character—are a subject which has never yet engaged the serious consideration of philosophers, though some opinion on it is implied in almost all modes of thinking on human character and education. And, I expect, that this will hereafter be regarded as a very important branch of study for practical purposes, and the more, in proportion as the weakening of positive beliefs respecting states of existence superior to the human, leaves the imagination of higher things less provided with material from the domain of supposed reality. To me it seems that human life, small and confined as it is, and as, considered merely in the present, it is likely to remain even when the progress of material and moral improvement may have freed it from the greater part of its present calamities, stands greatly in need of any wider range and greater height of aspiration for itself and its destination, which the exercise of imagination can yield to it without running counter to the evidence of fact; and that it is a part of wisdom to make the most of any, even small, probabilities on this subject, which furnish imagination with any footing to support itself upon. And I am satisfied that the cultivation of such a tendency in the imagination, provided it goes on *pari passu* with the cultivation of severe reason, has no necessary tendency to pervert the judgment; but that it is possible to form a perfectly sober estimate of the evidences on both sides of a question and yet to let the imagination dwell by preference on those possibilities, which are at once the most comforting and the most improving, without in the least degree overrating the solidity of the grounds for expecting that these rather than any others will be the possibilities actually realized.

Though this is not in the number of the practical maxims handed down by tradition and recognized as rules for the conduct of life, a great part of the happiness of life depends upon the tacit observance of it. What, for instance, is the meaning of that which is always accounted one of the chief blessings of life, a cheerful disposition? What but the tendency, either from constitution or habit, to dwell chiefly on the brighter side both of the present and of the future? If every aspect, whether agreeable or odious of every thing, ought to occupy exactly the same place in ou. imagination which it fills in fact, and therefore ought to fill in our deliberate reason, what we call a cheerful disposition would be but one of the forms of folly, on a par except in agreeableness with the opposite disposition in which the gloomy and painful view of all things is habitually predominant. But it is not found in practice that those who take life cheerfully are less alive to rational prospects of evil or danger and more careless of making due provision against them, than other people. The tendency is rather the other way, for a hopeful disposition gives a spur to the faculties and keeps all the active energies in good working order. When imagination and reason receive each its appropriate culture they do not succeed in usurping each other's prerogatives. It is not necessary for keeping up our conviction that we must die, that we should be always brooding over death. It is far better that we should think no further about what we cannot possibly avert, than is required for observing the rules of prudence in regard to our own life and that of others, and fulfilling whatever duties devolve upon us in contemplation of the inevitable event. The way to secure this is not to think perpetually of death, but to think perpetually of our duties, and of the rule of life. The true rule of practical wisdom is not that of making all the aspects of things equally prominent in our habitual contemplations, but of giving the greatest prominence to those of their aspects which depend on, or can be modified by, our own conduct. In things which do not depend on us, it is not solely for the sake of a more enjoyable life that the habit is desirable of looking at things and at mankind by preference on their pleasant side; it is also in order that we may be able to love them better and work with more heart for their improvement. To what purpose, indeed, should we feed our imagination with the unlovely aspect of persons and things? All *unnecessary* dwelling upon the evils of life is at best a useless expenditure of nervous force: and when I say unnecessary I mean all that is not necessary either in the sense of being unavoidable, or in that of being needed for the performance of our duties and for preventing our sense of the reality of those evils from becoming speculative and dim. But if it is often waste of strength to dwell on the evils of life, it is worse than waste to dwell habitually on its meannesses and basenesses. It is necessary to be aware of them; but to live in their contemplation makes it scarcely possible to keep up in oneself a high tone of mind. The imagination and feelings become tuned to a lower pitch; degrading instead of elevating associations become connected with the daily objects and incidents of life, and give their colour to the thoughts, just as associations of sensuality do in those who indulge freely in that sort of contemplations. Men have often felt what it is to have had their imaginations corrupted by one class of ideas, and I think they must have felt with the same kind of pain how the poetry is taken out of the things fullest of it, by mean associations, as when a beautiful air that had been associated with highly poetical words is heard sung with trivial and vulgar ones. All these things are said in mere illustration of the principle that in the regulation of the imagination literal truth of facts is not the only thing to be considered.

Truth is the province of reason, and it is by the cultivation of the rational faculty that provision is made for its being known always, and thought of as often as is required by duty and the circumstances of human life. But when the reason is strongly cultivated, the imagination may safely follow its own end, and do its best to make life pleasant and lovely inside the castle, in reliance on the fortifications raised and maintained by Reason round the outward bounds.

On these principles it appears to me that the indulgence of hope with regard to the government of the universe and the destiny of man after death, while we recognize as a clear truth that we have no ground for more than a hope, is legitimate and philosophically defensible. The beneficial effect of such a hope is far from trifling. It makes life and human nature a far greater thing to the feelings, and gives greater strength as well as greater solemnity to all the sentiments which are awakened in us by our fellow-creatures and by mankind at large. It allays the sense of that irony of Nature which is so painfully felt when we see the exertions and sacrifices of a life culminating in the formation of a wise and noble mind, only to disappear from the world when the time has just arrived at which the world seems about to begin reaping the benefit of it. The truth that life is short and art is long is from of old one of the most discouraging parts of our condition; this hope admits the possibility that the art employed in improving and beautifying the soul itself may avail for good in some other life, even when seemingly useless for this. But the benefit consists less in the presence of any specific hope than in the enlargement of the general scale of the feelings ; the loftier aspirations being no longer in the same degree checked and kept down by a sense of the insignificance of human life—by the disastrous feeling of 'not worth while.' The gain obtained in the increased inducement to cultivate the improvement of character up to the end of life, is obvious without being specified.

There is another and a most important exercise of imagination which, in the past and present, has been kept up principally by means of religious belief and which is infinitely precious to mankind, so much so that human excellence greatly depends upon the sufficiency of the provision made for it. This consists of the familiarity of the imagination with the conception of a morally perfect Being, and the habit of taking the approbation of such a Being as the *norma* or standard to which to refer and by which to regulate our own characters and lives. This idealization of our standard of excellence in a Person is quite possible, even when that Person is conceived as merely imaginary. But religion, since the birth of Christianity, has inculcated the belief that our highest conceptions of combined wisdom and goodness exist in the concrete in a living Being who has his eyes on us and cares for our good. Through the darkest and most corrupt periods Christianity has raised this torch on high—has kept this object of veneration and imitation before the eyes of man. True, the image of perfection has been a most imperfect, and, in many respects a perverting and corrupting one, not only from the low moral ideas of the times, but from the mass of moral contradictions which the deluded worshipper was compelled to swallow by the supposed necessity of complimenting the Good Principle with the possession of infinite power. But it is one of the most universal as well as of the most surprising characteristics of human nature, and one of the most speaking proofs of the low stage to which the reason of mankind at large has ever yet advanced, that they are capable of overlooking any amount of either moral or intellectual contradictions and receiving into their minds propositions utterly inconsistent with one another, not only without being shocked by the contradiction, but without preventing both the contradictory beliefs from producing a part at least of their natural consequences in the mind. Pious men and women have gone on ascribing to God particular acts and a general course of will and conduct incompatible with even the most ordinary and limited conception of moral goodness, and have had their own ideas of morality, in many important

particulars, totally warped and distorted, and notwithstanding this have continued to conceive their God
as clothed with all the attributes of the highest ideal
goodness which their state of mind enabled them to
conceive, and have had their aspirations towards
goodness stimulated and encouraged by that conception. And, it cannot be questioned that the un-
doubting belief of the real existence of a Being who
realizes our own best ideas of perfection, and of our
being in the hands of that Being as the ruler of the
universe, gives an increase of force to these feelings
beyond what they can receive from reference to a
merely ideal conception.

This particular advantage it is not possible for
those to enjoy, who take a rational view of the nature
and amount of the evidence for the existence and
attributes of the Creator. On the other hand, they
are not encumbered with the moral contradictions
which beset every form of religion which aims at
justifying in a moral point of view the whole government of the world. They are, therefore, enabled to
form a far truer and more consistent conception of
Ideal Goodness, than is possible to any one who
thinks it necessary to find ideal goodness in an omnipotent ruler of the world. The power of the Creator
once recognized as limited, there is nothing to disprove the supposition that his goodness is complete
and that the ideally perfect character in whose like-

ness we should wish to form ourselves and to whose supposed approbation we refer our actions, may have a real existence in a Being to whom we owe all such good as we enjoy.

Above all, the most valuable part of the effect on the character which Christianity has produced by holding up in a Divine Person a standard of excellence and a model for imitation, is available even to the absolute unbeliever and can never more be lost to humanity. For it is Christ, rather than God, whom Christianity has held up to believers as the pattern of perfection for humanity. It is the God incarnate, more than the God of the Jews or of Nature, who being idealized has taken so great and salutary a hold on the modern mind. And whatever else may be taken away from us by rational criticism, Christ is still left; a unique figure, not more unlike all his precursors than all his followers, even those who had the direct benefit of his personal teaching. It is of no use to say that Christ as exhibited in the Gospels is not historical and that we know not how much of what is admirable has been superadded by the tradition of his followers. The tradition of followers suffices to insert any number of marvels, and may have inserted all the miracles which he is reputed to have wrought. But who among his disciples or among their proselytes was capable of inventing the sayings ascribed to Jesus or of imagining the life and character revealed in the

Gospels ?   Certainly not the fishermen of Galilee ;
as certainly not St. Paul, whose character and
idiosyncrasies were of a totally different sort ; still
less the early Christian writers in whom nothing
is more evident than that the good which was in them
was all derived, as they always professed that it was
derived, from the higher source.   What *could* be
added and interpolated by a disciple we may see in the
mystical parts of the Gospel of St. John, matter im-
ported from Philo and the Alexandrian Platonists and
put into the mouth of the Saviour in long speeches
about himself such as the other Gospels contain not
the slightest vestige of, though pretended to have
been delivered on occasions of the deepest interest and
when his principal followers were all present ; most
prominently at the last supper.   The East was full
of men who could have stolen any quantity of this
poor stuff, as the multitudinous Oriental sects of
Gnostics afterwards did.   But about the life and sayings of Jesus there is a stamp of personal originality
combined with profundity of insight, which if we
abandon the idle expectation of finding scientific
precision where something very different was aimed
at, must place the Prophet of Nazareth, even in the
estimation of those who have no belief in his inspiration, in the very first rank of the men of sublime
genius of whom our species can boast.   When this
pre-eminent genius is combined with the qualities of

probably the greatest moral reformer, and martyr to
that mission, who ever existed upon earth, religion
cannot be said to have made a bad choice in pitching
on this man as the ideal representative and guide of
humanity; nor, even now, would it be easy, even
for an unbeliever, to find a better translation of the
rule of virtue from the abstract into the concrete, than
to endeavour so to live that Christ would approve our
life. When to this we add that, to the conception of
the rational sceptic, it remains a possibility that Christ
actually was what he supposed himself to be—not
God, for he never made the smallest pretension to
that character and would probably have thought such
a pretension as blasphemous as it seemed to the men
who condemned him—but a man charged with a
special, express and unique commission from God to
lead mankind to truth and virtue; we may well
conclude that the influences of religion on the character
which will remain after rational criticism has done its
utmost against the evidences of religion, are well
worth preserving, and that what they lack in direct
strength as compared with those of a firmer belief, is
more than compensated by the greater truth and
rectitude of the morality they sanction.

Impressions such as these, though not in themselves amounting to what can properly be called a
religion, seem to me excellently fitted to aid and
fortify that real, though purely human religion, which

sometimes calls itself the Religion of Humanity and sometimes that of Duty. To the other inducements for cultivating a religious devotion to the welfare of our fellow-creatures as an obligatory limit to every selfish aim, and an end for the direct promotion of which no sacrifice can be too great, it superadds the feeling that in making this the rule of our life, we may be co-operating with the unseen Being to whom we owe all that is enjoyable in life. One elevated feeling this form of religious idea admits of, which is not open to those who believe in the omnipotence of the good principle in the universe, the feeling of helping God—of requiting the good he has given by a voluntary co-operation which he, not being omnipotent, really needs, and by which a somewhat nearer approach may be made to the fulfilment of his purposes. The conditions of human existence are highly favourable to the growth of such a feeling inasmuch as a battle is constantly going on, in which the humblest human creature is not incapable of taking some part, between the powers of good and those of evil, and in which every even the smallest help to the right side has its value in promoting the very slow and often almost insensible progress by which good is gradually gaining ground from evil, yet gaining it so visibly at considerable intervals as to promise the very distant but not uncertain final victory of Good. To do something during life, on even the humblest scale if nothing

more is within reach, towards bringing this con-
summation ever so little nearer, is the most animating
and invigorating thought which can inspire a human
creature; and that it is destined, with or without
supernatural sanctions, to be the religion of the
Future I cannot entertain a doubt. But it appears
to me that supernatural hopes, in the degree and
kind in which what I have called rational scepticism
does not refuse to sanction them, may still con-
tribute not a little to give to this religion its due
ascendancy over the human mind.

FINIS

# GREAT BOOKS IN PHILOSOPHY PAPERBACK SERIES

## ETHICS

| | |
|---|---|
| Aristotle—*The Nicomachean Ethics* | $8.95 |
| Marcus Aurelius—*Meditations* | 5.95 |
| Jeremy Bentham—*The Principles of Morals and Legislation* | 8.95 |
| John Dewey—*The Moral Writings of John Dewey, Revised Edition* | |
| (edited by James Gouinlock) | 11.95 |
| Epictetus—*Enchiridion* | 4.95 |
| Immanuel Kant—*Fundamental Principles of the Metaphysic of Morals* | 5.95 |
| John Stuart Mill—*Utilitarianism* | 5.95 |
| George Edward Moore—*Principia Ethica* | 8.95 |
| Friedrich Nietzsche—*Beyond Good and Evil* | 8.95 |
| Plato—*Protagoras, Philebus,* and *Gorgias* | 7.95 |
| Bertrand Russell—*Bertrand Russell On Ethics, Sex, and Marriage* | |
| (edited by Al Seckel) | 19.95 |
| Arthur Schopenhauer—*The Wisdom of Life* and *Counsels and Maxims* | 7.95 |
| Benedict de Spinoza—*Ethics* and *The Improvement of the Understanding* | 9.95 |

## SOCIAL AND POLITICAL PHILOSOPHY

| | |
|---|---|
| Aristotle—*The Politics* | 7.95 |
| Francis Bacon—*Essays* | 6.95 |
| Mikhail Bakunin—*The Basic Bakunin: Writings, 1869–1871* | |
| (translated and edited by Robert M. Cutler) | 11.95 |
| Edmund Burke—*Reflections on the Revolution in France* | 7.95 |
| John Dewey—*Freedom and Culture* | 10.95 |
| G. W. F. Hegel—*The Philosophy of History* | 9.95 |
| G. W. F. Hegel—*Philosophy of Right* | 9.95 |
| Thomas Hobbes—*The Leviathan* | 7.95 |
| Sidney Hook—*Paradoxes of Freedom* | 9.95 |
| Sidney Hook—*Reason, Social Myths, and Democracy* | 11.95 |
| John Locke—*Second Treatise on Civil Government* | 5.95 |
| Niccolo Machiavelli—*The Prince* | 5.95 |
| Karl Marx—*The Poverty of Philosophy* | 7.95 |
| Karl Marx/Frederick Engels—*The Economic and Philosophic Manuscripts of 1844* | |
| and *The Communist Manifesto* | 6.95 |
| John Stuart Mill—*Considerations on Representative Government* | 6.95 |
| John Stuart Mill—*On Liberty* | 5.95 |
| John Stuart Mill—*On Socialism* | 7.95 |
| John Stuart Mill—*The Subjection of Women* | 5.95 |
| Friedrich Nietzsche—*Thus Spake Zarathustra* | 9.95 |
| Thomas Paine—*Common Sense* | 6.95 |
| Thomas Paine—*Rights of Man* | 7.95 |
| Plato—*Lysis, Phaedrus,* and *Symposium* | 6.95 |
| Plato—*The Republic* | 9.95 |
| Jean-Jacques Rousseau—*The Social Contract* | 5.95 |
| Mary Wollstonecraft—*A Vindication of the Rights of Men* | 5.95 |
| Mary Wollstonecraft—*A Vindication of the Rights of Women* | 6.95 |

## METAPHYSICS/EPISTEMOLOGY

| | |
|---|---|
| Aristotle—*De Anima* | 6.95 |
| Aristotle—*The Metaphysics* | 9.95 |
| George Berkeley—*Three Dialogues Between Hylas and Philonous* | 5.95 |
| René Descartes—*Discourse on Method* and *The Meditations* | 6.95 |
| John Dewey—*How We Think* | 10.95 |
| John Dewey—*The Influence of Darwin on Philosophy and Other Essays* | 11.95 |
| Epicurus—*The Essential Epicurus: Letters, Principal Doctrines, Vatican Sayings, and Fragments* (translated, and with an introduction, by Eugene O'Connor) | 5.95 |
| Sidney Hook—*The Quest for Being* | 11.95 |
| David Hume—*An Enquiry Concerning Human Understanding* | 6.95 |
| David Hume—*Treatise of Human Nature* | 9.95 |
| William James—*The Meaning of Truth* | 11.95 |
| William James—*Pragmatism* | 7.95 |
| Immanuel Kant—*Critique of Practical Reason* | 7.95 |
| Immanuel Kant—*Critique of Pure Reason* | 9.95 |
| Gottfried Wilhelm Leibniz—*Discourse on Method* and the *Monadology* | 6.95 |
| John Locke—*An Essay Concerning Human Understanding* | 9.95 |
| Plato—*The Euthyphro, Apology, Crito, and Phaedo* | 5.95 |
| Bertrand Russell—*The Problems of Philosophy* | 8.95 |
| George Santayana—*The Life of Reason* | 9.95 |
| Sextus Empiricus—*Outlines of Pyrrhonism* | 8.95 |

## PHILOSOPHY OF RELIGION

| | |
|---|---|
| Marcus Tullius Cicero—*The Nature of the Gods* and *On Divination* | 6.95 |
| Ludwig Feuerbach—*The Essence of Christianity* | 8.95 |
| David Hume—*Dialogues Concerning Natural Religion* | 5.95 |
| John Locke—*A Letter Concerning Toleration* | 5.95 |
| Lucretius—*On the Nature of Things* | 7.95 |
| John Stuart Mill—*Three Essays on Religion* | 7.95 |
| Thomas Paine—*The Age of Reason* | 13.95 |
| Bertrand Russell—*Bertrand Russell On God and Religion* (edited by Al Seckel) | 19.95 |

## ESTHETICS

| | |
|---|---|
| Aristotle—*The Poetics* | 5.95 |
| Aristotle—*Treatise on Rhetoric* | 7.95 |

## GREAT MINDS PAPERBACK SERIES

## ECONOMICS

| | |
|---|---|
| Charlotte Perkins Gilman—*Women and Economics: A Study of the Economic Relation between Women and Men* | 11.95 |
| John Maynard Keynes—*The General Theory of Employment, Interest, and Money* | 11.95 |
| Alfred Marshall—*Principles of Economics* | 11.95 |
| David Ricardo—*Principles of Political Economy and Taxation* | 10.95 |
| Adam Smith—*Wealth of Nations* | 9.95 |
| Thorstein Veblen—*The Theory of the Leisure Class* | 11.95 |

## RELIGION

| | |
|---|---|
| Thomas Henry Huxley—*Agnosticism and Christianity and Other Essays* | 10.95 |
| Ernest Renan—*The Life of Jesus* | 11.95 |
| Voltaire—*A Treatise on Toleration and Other Essays* | 8.95 |

## SCIENCE

Nicolaus Copernicus—*On the Revolutions of Heavenly Spheres*     8.95
Charles Darwin—*The Descent of Man*     18.95
Charles Darwin—*The Origin of Species*     10.95
Albert Einstein—*Relativity*     8.95
Michael Faraday—*The Forces of Matter*     8.95
Galileo Galilei—*Dialogues Concerning Two New Sciences*     9.95
Ernst Haeckel—*The Riddle of the Universe*     11.95
William Harvey—*On the Motion of the Heart and Blood in Animals*     9.95
Julian Huxley—*Evolutionary Humanism*     10.95
Edward Jenner—*Vaccination against Smallpox*     5.95
Johannes Kepler—*Epitome of Copernican Astronomy and Harmonies of the World*     8.95
Isaac Newton—*The Principia*     14.95
Louis Pasteur and Joseph Lister—*Germ Theory and Its Application to Medicine
 and On the Antiseptic Principle of the Practice of Surgery*     7.95
Alfred Russel Wallace—*Island Life*     16.95

## HISTORY

Edward Gibbon—*On Christianity*     9.95
Herodotus—*The History*     13.95
Thucydides—*History of the Peloponnesian War*     15.95
Andrew D. White—*A History of the Warfare of Science
 with Theology in Christendom*     19.95

## SOCIOLOGY

Emile Durkheim—*Ethics and the Sociology of Morals*
 (translated with an introduction by Robert T. Hall)     8.95

## CRITICAL ESSAYS

Desiderius Erasmus—*The Praise of Folly*     9.95
Jonathan Swift—*A Modest Proposal and Other Satires*
 (with an introduction by George R. Levine)     8.95
H. G. Wells—*The Conquest of Tme*
 (with an introduction by Martin Gardner)     8.95

*(Prices subject to change without notice.)*

# ORDER FORM

**Prometheus Books**
59 John Glenn Drive • Amherst, New York 14228–2197
Telephone: (716) 691–0133

**Phone Orders (24 hours):**
Toll free (800) 421–0351 • FAX (716) 691–0137
Email: PBooks6205@aol.com

Ship to: _____

Address _____

_____

City _____

County (*N.Y. State Only*) _____

Telephone _____

Prometheus Acct. # _____

❑ Payment enclosed (or)

Charge to ❑ VISA ❑ MasterCard

A/C: ☐☐☐☐☐☐☐☐☐☐☐☐☐☐☐☐☐☐☐☐

Exp. Date _____ / _____

Signature _____